AD Architectural Design

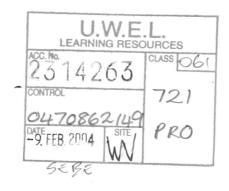

Property Development and Progressive Architecture: The New Alliance

Guest-edited by David B Sokol

W WILEY-ACADEMY

Architectural Design

Vol 74   No 1   January/February 2004

ISBN 0-470-86214-9
Profile No 167

Editorial Offices
International House
Ealing Broadway Centre
London W5 5DB
T: +44 (0)20 8326 3800
F: +44 (0)20 8326 3801
E: architecturaldesign@wiley.co.uk

Editor
Helen Castle
Production
Mariangela Palazzi-Williams
Art Director
Christian Küsters ↘ CHK Design
Designer
Scott Bradley ↘ CHK Design
**Project Coordinator
& Picture Editor**
Caroline Ellerby

Advertisement Sales
01243 843272

Editorial Board
Will Alsop, Denise Bratton,
Adriaan Beukers, André Chaszar,
Peter Cook, Teddy Cruz,
Max Fordham, Massimiliano Fuksas,
Edwin Heathcote, Anthony Hunt,
Charles Jencks, Jan Kaplicky,
Robert Maxwell, Jayne Merkel,
Monica Pidgeon, Antoine Predock,
Michael Rotondi, Leon van Schaik,
Kenneth Yeang

Contributing Editors
André Chaszar
Craig Kellogg
Jeremy Melvin
Jayne Merkel

Abbreviated positions
b=bottom, c=centre, l=left, r=right

Front and back cover: The Porter House, under
construction, in the Meatpacking District of
New York, which is designed and co-developed
by New York architects SHoP/Sharples Holden
Pasquarelli. Photo: © David Sokol.

AD

p 4 © Foster and Partners, photo Nigel Young;
pp 6 & 12 © Peter Aaron/Esto; p 9 (l) courtesy
Richard Meier & Partners, © Zhonggui Zhao;
p9 (br) © Scott Frances/Esto; p 10 © Norman
McGrath; p 11 courtesy Michael Graves &
Associates; p 14 © Jock Pottle/Esto; pp 16–19
© SHoP Architects; pp 20–1 © atelier BUILD,
photos Mathieu Manikowski; p 22(tl) © atelier
BUILD, photo Michael Carroll; pp 22(tr & br) &
23(tr) © atelier BUILD, photos Brigitte
Desrochers; pp 24 & 25 © atelier BUILD; pp
26–7 © Paul Warchol Photography; p 28 ©
Mick Hales; pp 29–31 © Eduard Hueber; pp
32–3 © Paul Stevenson Oles/Advanced Media
Design; pp 34 & 36–9 © Archi-Tectonics; p 35
© Paul Warchol Photography; pp 40–5 © Neal
E Jones, photos Timothy Hursley; p 46(l) ©
British Land; p 46(r) and 47(l) © Wordsearch,
photos Tim Motion; p 47(r) © Arup Associates;
pp 48 & 50 © Wordsearch; p 49 © Wordsearch,
photo Simon Hazelgrove; pp 51–7 © T R
Hamzah & Yeang Sdn Bhd; pp 59–61 ©
Hiroyuki Hori/Linea; pp 62–5 © Isao
Imbe/Takagi Planning; pp 66–7 © Atsushi
Matsuo; pp 68–9 & 71–3 © Patrick Bingham-
Hall; pp 74 & 79(bl & r) ©Stephen Varady; pp
75, 76(l), 77(br) & 78(t) © John Gollings; pp
76(r) & 79(tl) © Robert Nation;

p 77(t, bl and cr) 3DD Ltd; p 78(b) © Jan
Matuszczak; p 80 Images by Bozig; pp 81–7 ©
Gutierrez and Portefaix; pp 88–91 © West
8/Jeroen Musch; p 92 courtesy of De
Architekten Cie, © Jeroen Musch; p 93 © Ger
van der Vlugt; pp 95–9 © City of Malmö, photos
Jens Lindhe.

AD+

pp 102 & 104–05 © Austrian Cultural Forum,
photos Robert Polidori; pp 106 & 108(t) © Patel
Taylor, photos Michael Kaner; pp 108(bl & r) &
109 © Patel Taylor, photos Martin Charles;pp
110 courtesy Michael Graves; p 111 (l) photo A
Aubrey Bodine; (c) courtesy Charles Jencks,
photo Richard Bryant; (r) book cover photo
Balthazar Korab; pp 112–16 © Shahin Vassigh;
p 117 © estudio teddy cruz, photo Ana Alamán;
pp 118–24 © estudio teddy cruz; p 126 ©
Stephen Bram.

Published in Great Britain in 2004 by Wiley-
Academy, a division of John Wiley & Sons Ltd
Copyright © 2004, John Wiley & Sons Ltd, The
Atrium, Southern Gate, Chichester, West Sussex
PO19 8SQ, England, Telephone (+44) 1243 779777
Email (for orders and customer service enquiries):
cs-books@wiley.co.uk Visit our Home Page on
www.wileyeurope.com or www.wiley.com

All Rights Reserved. No part of this publication
may be reproduced, stored in a retrieval system
or transmitted in any form or by any means,
electronic, mechanical, photocopying, recording,
scanning or otherwise, except under the terms
of the Copyright, Designs and Patents Act 1988
or under the terms of a licence issued by the
Copyright Licensing Agency Ltd, 90 Tottenham
Court Road, London W1T 4LP, UK, without the
permission in writing of the Publisher.

Requests to the Publisher should be addressed
to the Permissions Department, John Wiley &
Sons Ltd, The Atrium, Southern Gate, Chichester,
West Sussex PO19 8SQ, England, or emailed to
permreq@wiley.co.uk, or faxed to (+44) 1243 770571.

Subscription Offices UK
John Wiley & Sons Ltd.
Journals Administration Department
1 Oldlands Way, Bognor Regis
West Sussex, PO22 9SA
T: +44 (0)1243 843272
F: +44 (0)1243 843232
E: cs-journals@wiley.co.uk

Annual Subscription Rates 2004
Institutional Rate: UK £175
Personal Rate: UK £99
Student Rate: UK £70
Institutional Rate: US $270
Personal Rate: US $155
Student Rate: US $110
AD is published bi-monthly.
Prices are for six issues and include
postage and handling charges.
Periodicals postage paid at Jamaica,
NY 11431. Air freight and mailing
in the USA by Publications
Expediting Services Inc, 200 Meacham
Avenue, Elmont, NY 11003

Single Issues UK: £22.50
Single Issues outside UK: US $45.00
Details of postage and packing charges
available on request

Postmaster
Send address changes to AD Publications
Expediting Services, 200 Meacham Avenue,
Elmont, NY 11003

Printed in Italy. All prices are subject to
change without notice. [ISSN: 0003-8504]

Property Development and Progressive Architecture:
The New Alliance
Guest-edited by David B Sokol

When John Ritblat, the chairman of one of the UK's largest property groups, British Land, declares that he would like to work with Frank Gehry or Herzog & de Meuron, it is apparent that something is afoot. Developers are openly looking beyond the 'safe hands' of corporate architectural practices to inject more sophisticated design values into their schemes. The catalyst for this change has, to some extent, got to be economic. The housing boom in many leading world cities, such as London, New York and Tokyo, has made the input of architects' skills more viable and more valuable. The employment of architects' spatial skills can often aid the feasibility of a project on a tight site. At the top of the housing market, higher-spec schemes with the tag of a signature architects' name can provide marketing leverage. However, the shift is also cultural. It is a reflection of the fact that there is a widening public and commercial appreciation for what architecture can do. Just as in the last few years Prada has realised the potential added value that high-profile architecture can bring to its brand, so has an insurance company like Swiss Re. Its iconic gherkin building is a sophisticated hoarding — a veritable presence throughout the City and on London's skyline. It is a masthead not only for the company, but also for the vitality of the City as it vies with Canary Wharf as London's financial centre. It is a device that the pioneer housing association Peabody Trust is using in a very different context. The trust builds architect-designed towers into its schemes in order to imbue confidence in the local community and send out messages that an area is being regenerated.

In many ways we are playing devil's advocate in this issue. You may not agree with our catholic definition of 'progressive architecture' and you certainly many not agree with our slightly one-sided, rose-tinted view — presented through so many success stories. (Every architect has his or her own cachet of developer horror stories.) As historically the odds have been so stacked against a fertile partnership between developer and architect, it was our aim here to look beyond the traditional impasse that existed between the two parties and explode the myth that it had to be a relationship wrought out of animosity. Guest-editor David Sokol has brought together an intriguing and diverse set of case studies — in terms of their scale, approach and geography. He has effectively shown what is possible when armed with endless stamina, financial nouse, patience and negotiating skills. As developer Jonathon Carroll so pertinently advocates in his interview with Sokol, there has to be 'a middle ground' that is able to transcend developers' suspicions that architects really want to be artists and, in turn, architects' suspicions that developers are out to make a quick buck regardless of their design input. △

Foster and Partners, 30 St Mary Axe, City of London, 1997–2004 Built on the site of the former Baltic Exchange, the architects are able to claim that this is 'the capital's first environmentally progressive tall building'. The Swiss Reinsurance Company is both the client and developer. The building is designed to accommodate office space for rent, as well as a head office for the company's own staff.

Building apartments in Manhattan is not for the faint of heart. Construction costs are astronomical because of the high costs of land, workers' wages, delivering materials on crowded streets and borrowed money, as the construction process can take up to five years. And the Byzantine array of zoning codes, building regulations and access requirements is so formidable that most architects hire 'expediters' (often architects who specialise in navigating the murky waters of New York City's building department) just to get the necessary permits. Plans are reviewed by the city planning commission, community boards, planning review boards; commissioners are impressed by a name, and a gifted architect may even be able to figure out a way to meet the requirements in an artful way.

This probably explains why Related Companies hired Robert A M Stern Architects to design Tribeca Park, an enormous building with 396 rental apartments, completed in 1999, in Battery Park City, a new neighbourhood with a complicated set of design guidelines enforced by the public authority with jurisdiction over the land. It may also be one of the reasons why RFR/Davis & Partners hired Michael Graves to design the Impala, a three-building mixed-use complex in two different zoning districts on the

Architecture in Developer Land

In a city with several thousand practising architects and hundreds of quite talented ones, two or three little-known specialists have been designing the lion's share of new apartments for decades. But now there are new apartment towers on the horizon by Michael Graves, Richard Meier and Robert A M Stern. **Jayne Merkel** looks into what their presence means for housing options and the skyline of New York City.

Opposite
Robert A M Stern Architects, Tribeca Park, Battery Park City, New York, 1999
A 435,000-square-foot building with 396 rental apartments and 117 parking spaces on the north end of Battery Park City, Tribeca Park is a short walk from where the World Trade Center stood. Costas Kondylis, who designs more New York City apartments than anyone else, was responsible for the apartment plans. The design was complicated due to the size of the project, the fact that the neighbourhood was still being developed and the existence of design guidelines. The scheme consists of a curved bar on the western edge facing the Hudson River stepping up to a 27-storey tower at the end of the block, down again around the corner, before becoming a loggia to enclose a garden.

landmarks officials and other groups. This is a process that deters all but the bravest, so it is hardly surprising that there has been a distinct lack of ambitious architecture since the 1920s. An ongoing housing shortage and the role of New York as a global city have only exasperated the situation; buyers have been snapping up whatever is there.

Still, there is competition. Using a star architect can raise the price of an apartment and also help move a project through the

Upper East Side where outspoken neighbourhood advocates can hold up a project for years.

Related, a large, highly respected development company based in New York City, went on to commission Stern to design the Chatham, a high-end condominium on the Upper East Side, and the Westminster, a large rental building in trendy Chelsea. RFR/Davis again employed Graves for the design of the public spaces at the Century, a 23-storey rental apartment tower at 90th Street and First Avenue, as well as the bulk of 425 Fifth Avenue, a 56-storey mixed-use tower at 38th Street, and asked Stern to design the Seville just around the corner from the Impala. Meanwhile, another group, Richard Born with partners Ira Drukier and Philip Suarez, invited Richard Meier to build an unmatched pair of crystalline residential towers in Greenwich Village at 173 and 176 Perry Street. Though Meier had designed Suarez's Gramercy Park apartment 15 years earlier and created the first legal lofts in an industrial building only three blocks from Perry Street in 1969, the project represented his first new construction in Manhattan.

However, to say that these architects 'designed' the buildings mentioned above may be overstating the case. On developers' residential projects such as these, the architects are indeed responsible for the exteriors and the public areas but work alongside specialists who design the actual apartments (and also do the working drawings) to make the most of the space given esoteric code restrictions and to respond to the market. Their input varies greatly from developer to developer and from project to project.

Though the Born/Drukier/Suarez collaboration had previously been involved with a number of boutique hotels, they were not big residential developers with an established way of doing things, therefore Meier had full responsibility for his buildings. But what he designed was simply the shell, lobbies and a service core. The apartments were sold unfinished, like lofts in old industrial buildings sometimes are today, so Meier's involvement here was limited to the two loft-like one-bedrooms and a duplex he was commissioned to design by the buyers.

But as Stern has pointed out, there is nothing new about selling the spaces unfinished. In the 1920s, when many of the city's most sought-after apartments were built, it was not uncommon for co-operatives to sell only partly completed floors, allowing the buyers to bring in their own architects to design the spaces on them. However, these fancy apartment buildings were virtually private clubs, built and owned jointly by people who knew one another, who created residential corporations and purchased shares of the whole rather than the floors and walls they occupied.

Today, most new buildings are condominiums built by entrepreneurs for the open market, each physical unit being sold to the occupant (as opposed to the shares of stock in a co-op). Condominiums bring higher prices for comparable spaces because buyers know they are likely to be denied admission to a co-op if it is not their primary residence and if they have limited capital, or simply because a committee doesn't like them (the selection process is secret and co-op boards are not forced to give a reason for denying admission, though discrimination on ethnic grounds is illegal – but not unheard of).

Buildings from the 1920s are still highly prized because of their spacious interiors, use of natural materials, solid construction and historic detail, but they are impossible to replicate today at competitive prices. Real-estate ads note when an apartment is prewar as it is considered more desirable, partly because the building codes of the time required every room – even kitchens and bathrooms – to have a window.

Commissioning well-known architects is one way in which developers of modern buildings can compete with the historic properties on the market. Thus it is often assumed that developers want famous architects for the marketing value of their names,

Opposite
Richard Meier and Partners, 173 and 176 Perry Street, New York, 2000
The development consists of two polygonal 16-storey towers with one apartment per floor, though some buyers have purchased two or three and combined them. Each tower has a concrete service core on the east side containing a lift, staircases and mechanical services. Floor-to-ceiling glass walls face the Hudson River on the west, a little open space on one side and the matching tower on the other across Perry Street. An irregular grid of columns about 20 feet apart provides the main constraint within the 11-foot-tall open quadrangular spaces, which run parallel to the city grid on two sides and conform to the angle of the river edge on the other. Views out towards the river are breathtaking; views into the tower next door may be more entertaining.

Right
Robert A M Stern Architects, Tribeca Park, Battery Park City, New York, 1999
The plan of this enormous residential building curves around its waterside block to follow a curve in the Hudson River and create an interior courtyard for the residents.

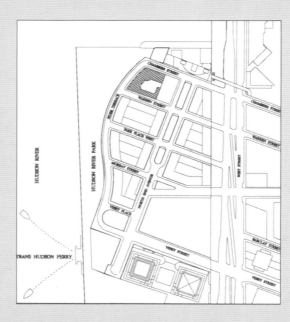

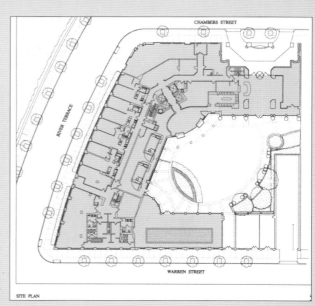

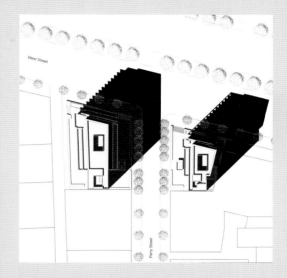

and ads that feature them serve only to fuel this suspicion. However, the developers say that what they are after is their expertise. 'I've always used great architects – for their talent,' says Trevor Davis, whose partners Aby Rosen and Michael Fuchs have been acquiring masterpieces of modern architecture, such as the Seagram Building and Lever House, the way some collectors buy paintings. 'I studied architecture and, you know, as the book *In Search of Excellence* says, it's always better to play tennis with somebody who's better than you are because you can rise up to that level.

'We try to choose the right architect for the right project,' Davis explained. 'In the case of the Impala we chose Michael Graves because I knew of his work on a project with three buildings and a large outdoor garden, and that was what we had there. And I was looking for something exuberant. I interviewed him and found him very tolerant. He was emphatic, not dogmatic. He was practical. He has a good business

head on him and he knows there are certain things developers have to do.'

But this doesn't mean he always likes it. Graves was disappointed when 'a small amount of decoration on the exterior of 425 Fifth Avenue which made the whole building make sense' was eliminated for budgetary reasons, though he is excited about the public spaces, which 'will be a knockout', and the exterior lighting that emphasises the tall slender tower's setbacks.

Graves explained why it is important that architects like himself are designing the apartment buildings of today: 'Eighty per cent of the buildings in New York are residential. That's what New York looks like.'

Stern also mentioned the impact on the streetscape: 'I like driving around in taxis and seeing my buildings.' And it seems others do, too. 'I got a call from a neighbour (because she'd seen the publicity and knew I lived there) saying that the lights on the west side of the Chatham had gone out and she missed them,' he said. She had gone to the right place. Stern called the developer and the lights were back on.

Stern's Tribeca Park bends along a curve in the Hudson River recalling the waterfront street wall of prewar apartments on the Upper West Side's Riverside Drive, culminating at the north end of the block with a 27-storey tower. The building has a 'variety of building heights', the architects explain, 'each responding to the scale of adjoining streets and future neighbours'. But the exterior treatment is simpler and flatter – with large windows, hard edges, bold overhangs and colossal columns – than the polite, small-scale, brick-and-stone facades of much of Battery Park City that

Above and right
Michael Graves & Associates and H Thomas O'Hara, the Impala, First Avenue, New York, 2000
The Impala consists of three adjoining red-brick, stone and precast-concrete buildings bridging two different zoning districts and surrounding a courtyard with a pool and garden. Retail and commercial spaces in the seven-storey base face First Avenue. There are medical offices on the 76th Street side and apartments on 75th Street. The rest of the complex's 204 rental unit apartments are located in a 24-storey tower that rises from the top of the base.

echo prewar buildings uptown. Its tougher, bolder vocabulary is intended to 'visually unite it with the nearby Tribeca warehouse district', while a wonderful loggia helps the building masses surround a garden at the centre of the site.

A few dozen blocks north on the Hudson River shore, Meier's transparent towers on Perry Street suggest another way to edge the river, more like Mies van der Rohe's approach for Chicago's Lake Shore Drive than anything in Manhattan. And with the opening of a new segment of the Hudson River Park, which will eventually extend all the way up the island, the towers are visible from the New York shoreline as well as from New Jersey and the river itself. Reflections from the water make the glass-walled towers, with white metal panels lining their edges and floor plates, seem all the more delicate, flanked as they are by solid brick industrial and apartment buildings. It's easy to imagine a whole row of elegant residential buildings following suit over time, especially as Meier's building sold quickly to glitterati such as Calvin Klein, Nicole Kidman and Martha Stewart at prices $1,000 a square foot higher than other apartments in the neighbourhood. (Meier himself owned a floor in the larger tower but decided not to move in because 'I don't have three years to spend designing an apartment and preparing for a move. I want to do other things with my time.')

The almost-twin towers (at 3,750 square feet, 173 Perry Street is actually about twice the size of 176 Perry Street) form a kind of gateway into the West Village, according to the architect. From the city side they create a portal into the new Hudson River Park across the busy West Side Highway. Once you manage to negotiate the traffic (there are stop-light buttons

Above and right
Michael Graves & Associates, 425 Fifth Avenue, New York, 2003
425 Fifth Avenue contains approximately 280,000 square feet of above-ground space with retail units, offices, shared recreational facilities and 46 floors of residential space. The first 17 floors are occupied by the extended-stay Envoy Club hotel's studios, one- and two-bedroom units of 550 to 1,250 square feet. On the upper floors there are 82 condominiums – studios, one-, two- and three-bedroom units that can easily be combined. Graves designed the oval foyer and elliptical lobby with Cipollino marble, burled Bosse Pomele wood and ebonised Santos rosewood. H Thomas O'Hara was associate architect.

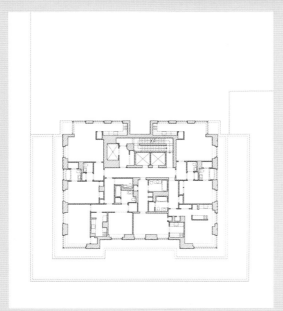

425 FIFTH AVENUE GROUND FLOOR PLAN

0   20   40 Feet

1. VESTIBULE
2. RESIDENTIAL LOBBY
3. ELEVATOR LOBBY
4. MAIL ROOM
5. RETAIL
6. OFFICE LOBBY
7. LOADING DOCK
8. PLAZA
9. GARDEN

FIFTH AVENUE

EAST 38TH STREET

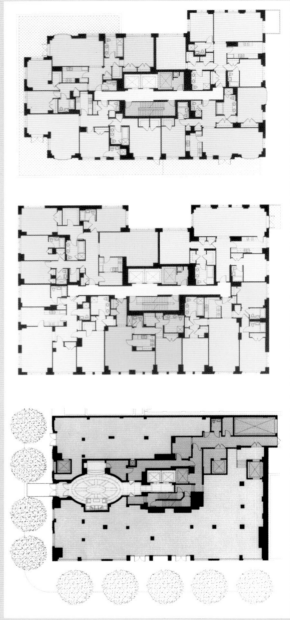

for pedestrians), there is a wonderful place to wander, cycle, fish, sit by the water and admire the buildings. From the interiors of the apartments the park provides a garden at the water's edge. Some of the grass here is bright-green Astroturf and the edges are very crisp, which led the architectural photographer Peter Aaron to observe during a shoot that from the towers this green space looks a little like a CAD drawing.

What Richard Born and partners have created here, however, is unique to New York, both in the streetscape and for the apartment market, since other projects by well-known architects are variations on, or expansions of, established types. However, it is not clear to what extent the shimmering towers will be able to maintain their uniform appearance once they are fully occupied, as although all of the units have grey solar blinds, owners may install curtains or blinds of their own inside them. When Mies built his first Lake Shore Drive towers he found that a disturbing irregular pattern resulted from the use of various curtains, so for the next pair of towers every apartment had curtains on two tracks running in tandem – the white ones that the building required for its uniformity on the outside and curtains of the tenants' choice on the inside.

In contrast, it won't much matter what occupants of Graves's 425 Fifth Avenue do with their window treatments as the slender yellow, dark-blue and white tower in midtown rises 671 feet over a block of relatively low-rise commercial lofts and stores, overlooking Lord & Taylor, the New York Public Library and Bryant Park, and beckoning to the Empire State Building four blocks south. Because it steps back in stages as if conforming to the zoning legislation that brought the city's great historic skyscrapers into existence, and has strong vertical bands of brick, it appears even taller and thinner than it actually is and resembles Hood, Godley & Fouilhoux's equally colourful and particularly handsome 33-storey McGraw-Hill Building of 1931 (on 42nd Street near Eighth Avenue). But this is very much a new mixed-use building type, with two floors of shops on Fifth Avenue and four floors of offices in its base, a floor filled with recreational facilities and an eighth-storey 'sky lobby' for the extended-stay hotel on the residential tower's lower floors.

Developers tend to place smaller apartments on the lower floors of apartment buildings where views are less spectacular and structural supports more intrusive, limiting planning possibilities. The spaces at Fifth Avenue proved a particular challenge for architect H Thomas O'Hara, responsible for the plans for all of the apartments Graves has worked on with RFR/Davis, as the structural frame for this very slim tower in a wind corridor was especially intrusive. (Developers prefer concrete to steel frames because they are quicker to build, labour costs are lower, and they allow slimmer floor plates. What space they lose in plan, they gain in elevation, and it is therefore possible to build more floors, with more dramatic views, within the same zoning envelope).

In addition, when marketing these buildings developers suddenly 'gain' even more floors, because it is conventional in New York to advertise an apartment that is actually only 50 storeys from the ground as being on, say, the 60th floor if it is at the same height as an apartment in a building with lower ceiling heights would be – just one of the mysteries of residential building in Manhattan. Every development company has its own way of doing things, which varies from building to building as does the relationship between the design architect and the building architect. At 425 Fifth Avenue, Graves designed the public spaces and the finishes and fixtures for the apartments, and landscape architect Thomas Balsley designed the little pocket park next to the condominium entrance on 38th Street.

Well-known architects, who tend to be perfectionists, naturally strive for as much control as possible, convinced they can make a difference. But they also understand the rules of the game. 'I'm not going to the mat over the location of the loo,' Stern said. But he did enjoy designing model apartments for various hypothetical tenants at Related's Westminster (which sold out quickly) and for a luxury apartment in the same company's ADL Time Warner headquarters building on Columbus Circle designed by Skidmore, Owings & Merrill (SOM).[1]

Relationships tend to work best when architects are involved early on. Stern enjoyed sitting around with the developers of the Chatham and their marketing consultant Louise Sunshine (of the Sunshine Group), who was also involved from the beginning, talking about who the apartments might appeal to and what these potential buyers might want.[2] 'Early in the process they were saying things like, if you are going to do three bedrooms, they're going to want a lavatory.'

Although Ismael Leyva Architects did the plans for the Chatham and the Westminster, Stern had some input, especially at the Chatham where he now lives (as do several of the partners of the development company). But did he imagine living there while he was working on the apartments? 'I've never designed a house that I didn't think I was going to move into,' he says.

There is extra room for innovation in the Chatham apartments, which real-estate brokers have rated the number-one new construction on the Upper East Side. The apartments, which were sold as condominiums, are large and varied in plan. Those designed for rental follow more of a formula, as people move in and out often and rarely redesign the apartments to their own specifications. They usually have very small rooms – as little space as possible to qualify as a one- or two-bedroom unit – which seem to be getting smaller all the time (though the Americans with Disabilities Act has meant that bathrooms are now larger).

Still, Related vice-chairman David Wine (in charge of design) says the company likes to offer as many types of plans as possible. And using different architects helps provide other options. Wine and Related chairman and CEO Stephen M Ross first met

Opposite
Robert A M Stern Architects with Ismael Leyva Architects, the Chatham, 65th Street and Third Avenue, New York, 2001
The Chatham recalls historic Park Avenue apartment buildings with a limestone facade on the first two floors of its base. But at 32 storeys it is twice as tall and its 94 condominium apartments are set back from the 85-foot base with shops on the ground floor, whereas the only commercial space in most prewar apartment buildings is devoted to doctors' offices. Limestone accents on the red-brick exterior, bay windows, French balconies and a decorative water tower nod to prewar neighbours, though the apartments have more expansive views and the building offers a wide variety of plans.

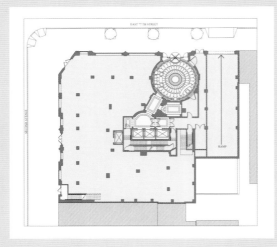

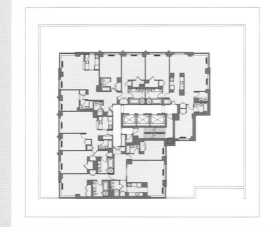

Robert A M Stern Architects
with SLCE (Schuman
Lichenstein Claman & Erron),
the Seville, Second Avenue,
New York, 2002

Far right
The Seville occupies an
L-shaped site at 77th Street
and Second Avenue. Originally
planned as a rental building,
this 31-storey tower was already
under construction when the
developers, RFR/Davis &
Partners, decided to make it
a condominium instead, so the
number of units was reduced to
170 and they were redesigned.
A few were sold unfinished to
buyers who wanted to
customise their apartments.
The building is clad in off-white
brick with black-brick vertical
accents. It steps back above a
base and has an Art Moderne
feel, but windows almost to the
floor and hard-edged
rectangular detailing make it of
our time. Stern likes to leave
some wall space at the end of
windows and room for valances
above them so that people who
install curtains don't have them
bunched up or hung in front
of glass. Here, panels above
the floor contain mechanical
services and avoid the need for
safety glass or guardrails which
are required when windows are
all the way to the floor.

Right, top
Ground-floor plan.

Right, bottom
Typical floor plan.

Stern in 1995 during a limited competition,
sponsored by the Municipal Art Society, for a
mixed-used building on Union Square. Though
Stern didn't get the job, he asked them to keep
him in mind. A little later: 'We were looking for
architects to submit schemes to the Battery
Park City Authority, and I received a call from
him saying he was still interested in doing
something with us. He reached out to me!'
says Wine, still surprised. Then, 'When we
saw Bob's scheme, I knew it was right.'

Ambitious architects and ambitious
developers may no longer be living in parallel
universes where the twain never meet, but the
complexity of building in Manhattan and the
stakes involved ensure that they are not likely
to be walking off into the sunset hand in hand
at any point in the near future.

'It goes down to economics. There is only
so much you can charge,' Stern explained.
'We've just designed a building in Vancouver,
13 storeys on the water. On each floor there is
one apartment with 4,000 square feet. On the
top there's a duplex with a double-height living
room. Every apartment is like a house. It's very
pricey to Vancouver, but I shudder to think what
it would cost here.'

Michael Graves & Associates, Proposed Residential Tower for White Plains, New York, in design
This mixed-use development is in an urban renewal district on Main Street in the downtown of a city in Westchester County, New York, within easy commuting distance of Manhattan. The 24-storey tower will contain 121 residential condominium units in a variety of configurations ranging from flexible lofts on floors 3 through to 5 to larger three- and four-bedroom apartments on the upper floors. Common space on the sixth floor will include a fitness centre, conference area, multipurpose room, pool and roof garden, with parking on the two basement levels. The first two floors of the approximately 260,000-square-foot complex will be devoted primarily to retail space. The tower will be set back on all sides from the base and massed in an elongated cruciform shape to emphasise the verticality of the structure while providing additional corner rooms to take advantage of the views over the city and the Hudson River. The condominiums are intended to appeal to a wide market, from younger singles and couples who want to live close to the commuter rail station to families and parents whose children have left home. The project is part of a trend to reurbanise larger towns and small cites in the New York metropolitan area around transit hubs.

Notes
1 Last summer David Martinez, a London-based financier, bought a 12,000-square-foot apartment on the 76th floor of the Time Warner Building for around $45 million.
2 Sunshine is involved in many high-end Manhattan projects and her marketing ability is a matter of more than projections. When selling the Perry Street apartments she moved the sales office into Richard Meier's office, way off the beaten track on West Tenth Street in midtown, because she realised that people who would be interested in them would be intrigued rather than put off by the glamorous office in a gritty industrial area.

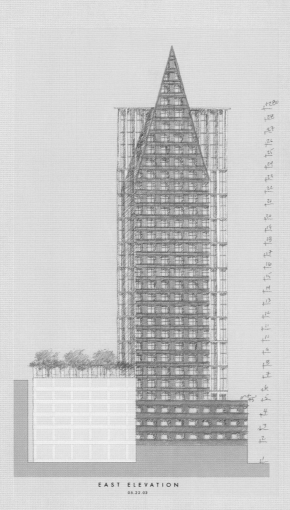

EAST ELEVATION
05.22.03

MAIN STREET ELEVATION
05.22.03

Graves thinks wistfully about a project he designed in the Hague for the Netherlands Ministry of Health, Welfare and Sport with developer Nanno Vaartjes. Although it was an office building (of about 96,000 square feet) and involved recladding a 19-storey jack-slab tower from the 1950s, it was part of the De Resident redevelopment district where new housing and other facilities were being built by Rob Krier, Cesar Pelli, Sjoerd Soeters, Adolfo Natalini, Karelse & Van der Meer and Gunnar Daan. 'We would meet, and everybody got to criticise everybody else's projects. It was as though we were in school, and it helped us make ours better. Everybody got his way, but his way was within boundaries.'

New York City may have been founded by the Dutch but Manhattan today is certainly not the Netherlands. Its dog-eat-dog ethic is almost the antithesis of civilised co-operation and much of its vitality comes from its crazy congestion, out-of-control capitalism and clash of competing interests, as Rem Koolhaas observed decades ago.

There is one little oasis, however, where the rules are completely different. Down in Battery Park City, which was built on landfill east of the Wall Street area in the 1970s when the corporate

and governmental ducks were all in a row (David Rockefeller was in charge at the Chase Manhattan Bank and his brother Nelson governor of New York), there is a public authority in charge – and there are design guidelines. A number of respected architects have designed buildings here. The area has been planned and replanned, and planned again, each time with new guidelines. Though none of the plans have as yet produced a lively neighbourhood, and the area remains slightly cut off from the rest of the city, Battery Park City does have a wonderful series of parks and waterfront promenades, ferry connections and the city's most sought-after public high school (where admission is by test score only). It has also served as a kind of testing ground for new ideas in a controlled environment. The latest effort is devoted to green construction, and Stern's next project for Related will be built here according to new green guidelines.

Graves is now working on another housing type new to the New York area – a pair of high-end residential towers in the middle of White Plains, a city in the middle of suburban Westchester County with commuter rail connections to New York City. And Richard Meier is already designing another building just a block south of his crystalline towers, the way Mies repeated his act on Lake Shore Drive, only this time he's designing the interiors too – a first for the New York apartment market. △

Calculated Risk

When there's nary a commission in sight, architecture's avant-garde is known to retreat to the world of paper. Not Sharples Holden Pasquarelli (SHoP). **Sara Moss** explains how even in the midst of a residential building boom in New York City, SHoP Architects has stayed true to its design mission by becoming its own client. With Jeffrey M Brown Associates, SHoP is partial owner of the Porter House, one of the newest residential buildings to grace the gritty but gentrifying streets of Manhattan's Meatpacking District. It may just serve as SHoP's business model hereafter, and one for other architects to emulate.

Opposite
View looking northeast from
the corner of Ninth Avenue
and 14th Street.

Right
View looking northeast of
the existing building before
renovation.

Below top
East (left) and north (right)
elevations, showing new and
old facades as well as the
elevator penthouse that tops
the addition.

Below bottom
West (left) and south (right)
elevations, showing the
pavement canopy and the
addition's 8-foot cantilever.

SHoP Architects could be a model firm for the future of architecture: computer-aided, sans conventional construction documents, seemingly unrealisable geometries and combinations. This is a doubly fitting crowning because unlike the stuff of paper dreams, the firm is busy executing designs. One of SHoP's current projects is the Porter House, a 10-storey residential conversion and addition in Manhattan's Meatpacking District. At a total cost of $22 million, it restores a 1905 brick Renaissance revival warehouse built for wine importers Julius Wile, and in its top two floors adds a rectilinear zinc-clad volume that extends four storeys above it and cantilevers 8 feet over a neighbouring roof.

From the exterior, the cantilevered addition appears to be a simple box. The complex way in which it fits back into the existing building, however, yields many permutations. Each apartment – there are 22 units in all – is a unique combination of old and new structure and skin. Sections of the apartments that are part of the addition are fitted with floor-to-ceiling windows; in several units that are part of the existing building, older curved window frames are preserved. And in one unit, the setback addition turns the building's original cornice into a balcony wall.

Meanwhile, the exterior zinc panel system is punctuated by inset light boxes. Combined with the glow from the apartments, these form a registration of light on the building's exterior that changes daily if not hourly, responding to the residents' comings and goings. The panels themselves will change over time in a far slower manner, the zinc weathering and growing richer in texture.

Structurally, simplicity is even more an appearance than a truth. The new reinforced concrete frame, built to support the cantilevered addition and bring the entire building up to seismic standards, will sit in the masonry of the existing six-storey building carved out to accommodate it. For additional support, small piles have been dug 70 feet deep into the bedrock below – half of them in tension, half in compression (SHoP enlisted Buro Happold as civil, structural and MEP engineers). The building originally had two cores in its corners, but to free up precious corner space these were removed and replaced with a new central lift and stair core.

And here's the catch. SHoP wasn't paid for its work until the apartments started selling.

SHoP worked with developer Jeffrey Brown for three months to design the Porter House completely on spec. Both SHoP and Brown are simultaneously the clients, developers, owners and marketers. They have conceived of and managed all aspects of the project, from designing a book about the building for prospective buyers, to negotiating with Design Within Reach to furnish the model apartments. As minority owners, SHoP will receive a percentage of the building's profits,

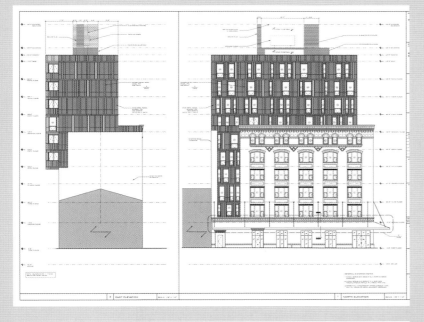

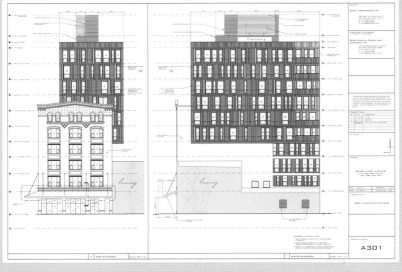

and hopes this will be one of many projects to be built this way. Gregg Pasquarelli, one of SHoP's five principals (along with Kim Holden, Bill Sharples, Chris Sharples and Coren Sharples) calls the Porter House's September 2003 opening 'the debut of our brand'.

The brand Pasquarelli is referring to is the way in which SHoP and Brown are getting buildings built. The architect is a service provider; the building, not simply the design, is the deliverable. Pasquarelli sees design as just one layer of the process of making buildings: 'There are so many other factors – legislative, economic, cultural, material,' he says. 'It's thinner than just doing the skin. Design is two per cent of what building is about.' This, too, could be the future of architecture.

Jeffrey Brown, a Philadelphia-based builder and developer, met the SHoP team several years ago while interviewing architects who he describes as the 'usual suspects – well-known and heavily experienced' residential architects. 'The truth,' says Brown, 'is that I didn't like anything that they were telling me. My approach is to produce the difference that makes the difference.' For Brown, the difference was design that he found exciting, produced at a lower cost. 'The more sophisticated buyers of our services – they are the ones who are starting to lean towards a design/build approach,' he adds.

While at first the two offices seem mismatched in scale – Brown has 150 employees while SHoP has a total of 16 – their attitudes are remarkably similar. Both men speak about their project, and about the process itself, with a rare enthusiasm. Says Brown of SHoP: 'I chose them for their energy. They have good positive energy.'

According to Pasquarelli, being your own client is both punishing and rewarding. One is setting one's own parameters and 'scripting rules', he says, and being so invested in the project makes SHoP more demanding of themselves. 'We're the hardest clients we've ever worked for,' Pasquarelli says.

However, it also has its advantages. Decision-making is relatively quick, communication is easier and all involved have the same interests, which is a change from the conventional dynamic: '[Usually] you have the owner, the builder and the architects,' says Brown, 'it's a triangle of built-in adversity.' But he is not interested in perpetuating that type of relationship: 'We like to assemble our team early and work intensely with them from the first minute.'

This approach has helped SHoP work with Brown from the beginning to design the building that they want instead of working on a design that is later compromised in order to cut costs. Confronting and incorporating economic or logistical realities at an early stage in a project turns potential limitations into strengths and allows architects to set their design priorities intelligently.

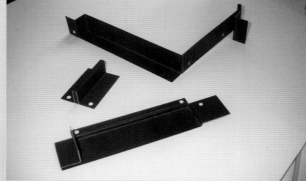

Building on spec also strengthens the relationship between the architects and the developer. 'In order to gain the trust of the client, in order to do more experimental work,' says Pasquarelli, 'you have to be willing to take the risk with the client, and you have to prove that higher risk leads to higher reward.'

The higher risk in this case is a design that combines luxurious materials and apartments, all of which are different combinations of new and old structure. Working in such a close, collaborative way has allowed SHoP to change what it needs to in order to get things done quickly and efficiently, and this has included conventional methods of communicating with those actually building the project. Construction drawings have included an isometric without dimensions demonstrating how the zinc panel cladding system will be put together, and instructions for cutting the panels from the standard sheet sizes so as to waste as little material as possible. 'As an architect, all you can do is to organise information and lay it out in an intelligent way, so that complex things become simple,' explains Pasquarelli.

Though this is the first project in which SHoP has been in an equity position, the team's attempt to rethink how architects work has been evolving throughout their work: 'In Greenport [a carousel house built in Greenport, Long Island, as part of a larger commission for redeveloping Mitchell Park] we met with every subcontractor and asked, how would you do this?'

While the Porter House may be smaller than Brown's other projects, he says. 'It's not so much the size as the ingredients'. This modestly sized building – a 30,000-square-foot renovation and 15,000-square-foot addition – will, Brown hopes, be 'adventurous and sympathetic at the same time. Most residential development is pretty unexciting. This building is exciting from both the interior and exterior.'

The Porter House's 22 units consist of five one-bedroom apartments, nine two-bedrooms, seven three-bedrooms and one four-bedroom penthouse duplex. Costs range from $735,000 for a one-bedroom, to $4.15 million for the four-bedroom apartment. Pasquarelli likens the current residential development industry to the booming boutique hotel industry of the 1980s and sees an opportunity in supplying design/build services to fill 'an unfulfilled niche of better product at a reasonable cost'. While forgoing a conventional fee may be risky, it not only yields a project that will go up quickly but gives him more control over the final product. 'I hope we get to the point where we never get paid a fee again,' he says. △

BUILDing Design

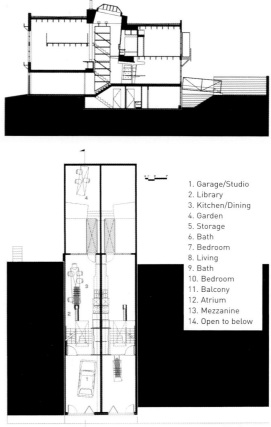

1. Garage/Studio
2. Library
3. Kitchen/Dining
4. Garden
5. Storage
6. Bath
7. Bedroom
8. Living
9. Bath
10. Bedroom
11. Balcony
12. Atrium
13. Mezzanine
14. Open to below

Sidewalk

David B Sokol describes the stripped-down oeuvre of Montreal-based BUILD. By transforming limitation into opportunities with a sense of both irony and fun, the firm makes it hard to discern that its method is rooted in fiscal responsibility.

BUILD, Thin House, Plateau
Mont-Royal, Montreal, 1996

Opposite
The rear elevation of Thin
House comprises corrugated
metal, which directly
references other city buildings
(city building codes stipulate
that only the front elevations
of buildings can be clad in
masonry) and particularly the
old sheds that housed firewood.

Above left
In addition to echoing the
neighbourhood's cornices,
Thin House is clad in contextual
brick in addition to concrete
block. The move allows a play
of colour and gives the building
a more domestic scale.

Top right
Plan and section.

In 1995 Quebec was on the verge of secession. Although the effort ultimately failed, Canadian citizens as well as investors feared the province's instability and migrated to Toronto. But Michael Carroll and Danita Rooyakkers stayed and founded design-development firm BUILD. Carroll explains that at the time 'it wasn't good for finding work in an office but it was good in terms of doing your own development, because the properties were devalued and the labour was fairly inexpensive'.

In Canada, multi-family construction loans are typically 75 per cent of total cost, and lenders require that developers pre-sell half of the units before ground breaking. So with Rooyakkers' family as the firm's initial financial backers instead, BUILD completed Thin House in 1996. Located in the Plateau Mont-Royal neighbourhood of Montreal, Thin House is an exploration of what Carroll calls 'critical dimension: in our discussions we really start with the idea of critical dimension – the idea of editing the building to a basic enclosure by eliminating mouldings, by trying to get something as clean and basic as possible, but still interesting.' To achieve that objective, for Thin House BUILD designed atrium-like spaces that prioritise the building's section and make its two units (at approximately 10.5 x 56 feet) feel larger than their plans might suggest.

Exterior details are chosen to effect a contextualism that is more ironic than historicist; for example, its folded metal cornices, hung along the taut concrete-block shell, glibly echo and continue the massing of surrounding buildings.

'Montreal is such a great city and has a very good fabric,' says Carroll, 'so we spend a lot of time cycling around the back lanes and looking at the odd things that happen with buildings; the boxes that line the back laneways, for example, all the metal. If you go down the back ways in Montreal, these metal sheds are the urban vernacular and there are a lot of spiral staircases and external balconies which are part of the whole street personality as well.'

Contextualism is just one localised circumstance to which the firm responds in its own style. For example, in the four-unit Tower House (1997), a fire escape was mandated by code. BUILD transformed it into a playful bridge device that visually connects the building's two tower-like volumes, rather than an ugly tack-on. The firm interprets what was, such as vernacular tropes, and what has to be, ie building codes.

In describing the fire escape, Carroll says that at one time he may have considered such necessities a compromise of creativity: 'I've worked in architecture offices, and I've found that everything tends to work down – by the time it's finished everybody wants to get away from it. Because we're involved in the construction of it and realisation of it, however, we have to build up to it. We can't arrive at a moment of depletion.'

Above left
BUILD, **Tower House, Plateau Mont-Royal, Montreal, 1997**
Tower House is indented to create an entry courtyard into a ground-floor unit, and visually separates the building into two tower-like volumes. Above the courtyard, a bridge serves as a playful fire escape (as per city building codes).

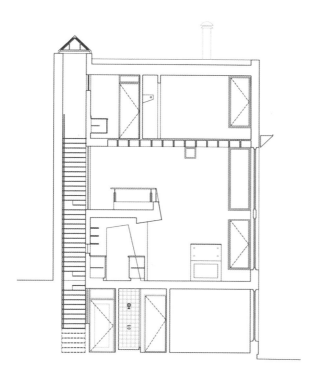

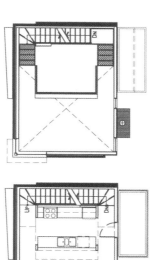

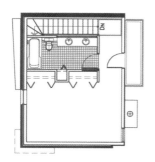

BUILD, **Box House, Plateau Mont-Royal, Montreal, 2000**

Opposite, top right
In order to add drama to the simple open-plan space, the struts supporting the living-room mezzanine lean into the living space.

Opposite, bottom right
Box House is wood-frame constructed, and towers above its single-storey neighbours.

Above, right
The back-door entry. This side elevation is sheathed in corrugated metal siding.

Above, left, bottom left and right
Section, floor plans and site plan.

BUILD, EcoCité Habitat I, Pointe
St Charles, Montreal, 2003

Above
Composite image showing the
southern facade of EcoCité.
The building's brise-soleil
continues the lines of the
neighbourhood balconies.
Although the facade is highly
glazed, vacuum-tube solar
collectors will be attached to
solid cladding to collect
sunlight, heating the building's
water system.

Opposite
EcoCité's volumetric strategy
is to bookend the
neighbourhood block and turn
it towards the adjacent park.

Carroll's description captures the architect-
cum-developer's perspective of design as
process. As he puts it: 'I think we really
emphasise the idea of building from the ground
up. The design is very much based on logistics
and pragmatics, and bylaws and those kinds
of things that everybody is dealing with. But
I think we start with the least we can do,
and what is absolutely essential, and how we
can develop the project so that it works
economically and we can do something
interesting in terms of design. So it's very kind
of base-level, and then we work up, which is
kind of refreshing because the project always
gets better than worse.'

These days BUILD also includes engineer
and contractor Attila Tolnai. The firm still
experiences limitations. For example, it
chooses only marginal or interstitial sites
for its projects, viewing them as affordable
investment opportunities. Its most recently
completed project, the single-family Box
House, is situated at the corner of an alleyway
and a narrow lane. Here, the lane is reduced
from two lanes to one, so that the building
appears to occupy the middle of the street.
Despite such challenges as narrow or

idiosyncratic sites, Carroll maintains that 'if you're
confident in what you're doing, the design process
can be much faster, which I think is an important test
of your intuition'.

A First Client
Rather than initiate and develop its own designs, BUILD
found its first client in Christopher Holmes. The firm's
design philosophy has not been compromised by the
relationship, however, because Holmes represents,
in his opinion, a new generation of both consumer
and developer. Holmes and BUILD have just finished
EcoCité Habitat I, an eight-unit condominium in
Montreal's Pointe St Charles neighbourhood, located
near the municipally redeveloped Canal Lachine and
in the first stages of gentrification. The vacant site is
adjacent to a baseball diamond, ostensibly providing
Holmes with a corner plot.

As the company name implies, EcoCité creates
'green' condominium development, or 'EcoCondos'
as Holmes calls them. Habitat I is well situated for
southern exposure, and consequently passive solar
heating will contribute greatly to the building's
warmth in the wintertime. Moreover, Carroll says
that solar vacuum tubes, which transfer energy to the
building's hot water, will clad portions of the exterior.
A geothermal pump will supply the remainder of the

heating requirements for the condominiums, as well as cooling.

Moreover, demonstrating that green design is as healthy for individual occupants as it is for the environment, each unit is provided with garden space either at ground level or on the rooftop. The building's brise-soleil, which in typical BUILD tradition echoes the balconies found throughout Montreal's urban fabric, can be outfitted with window-box planters providing south-facing occupants with further shade throughout the summer months.

Holmes has decided that a building that breathes differently from its neighbours should also stand apart from them architecturally. What Holmes has deemed 'eco chic', BUILD's Neo-Modernist design approach signifies EcoCité's ecological distinction. In addition, the pared-down aesthetic is commensurate with green building. For example, the ceilings expose the corrugated-steel pan that sits underneath concrete block. By not concealing the pan, the geothermal heating and cooling tubes just above can better radiate downwards into the living spaces. Further features compensate for the additional expenses of green building, such as contemporary MDF

cabinetry that replaces more typical woods to make up for the added cost of, say, grey-water recycling.

Even if prospective homeowners cannot comprehend the link between environmentalism and visual aesthetic, Holmes's total approach is founded on a belief that the Montreal residential market has matured. 'The majority of the real-estate market produces the exact same thing,' he says, 'so I felt that an integrated marketing concept could differentiate this from the market as a whole. Purely from a business strategy perspective, it makes a more durable, long-term strategy.'

And Holmes has other long-term plans: BUILD-designed EcoCité Habitat II, in the trendy Plateau Mont-Royal neighbourhood of Montreal, is under way, and larger projects are forthcoming. He has also trademarked the EcoCité and EcoCondo concepts in order to franchise them throughout North America, and for his forthcoming EcoCondo projects has resolved to continue his collaboration with BUILD.

However, this doesn't mean that BUILD won't be developing more of its own designs in the future. While Carroll admits that the firm's business strategy allowed it to 'build a portfolio of work' when commissions weren't available, persisting in self-development from single-family to multi-unit buildings 'enables us to have a freer range'. ∆

A Tower of Damnation

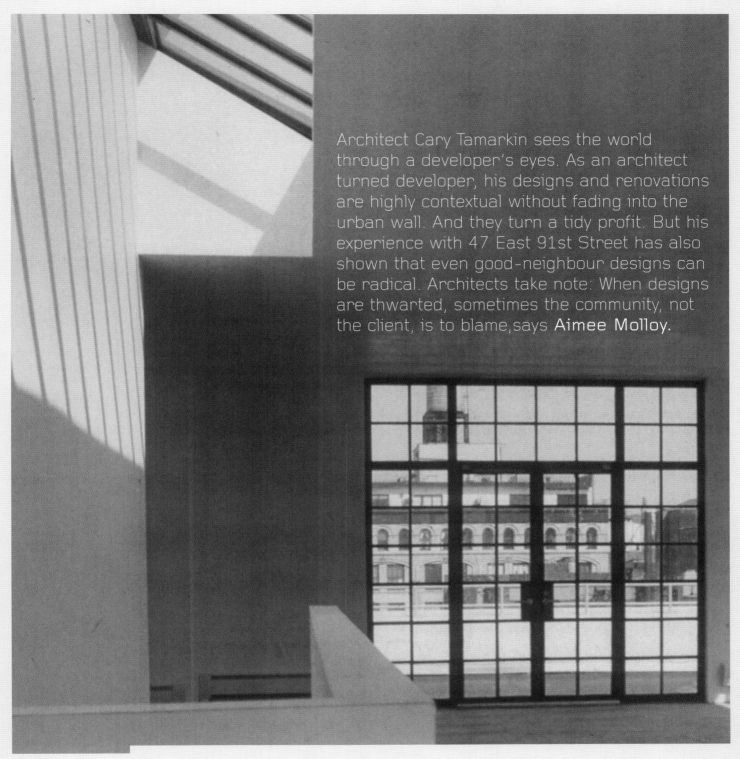

Architect Cary Tamarkin sees the world through a developer's eyes. As an architect turned developer, his designs and renovations are highly contextual without fading into the urban wall. And they turn a tidy profit. But his experience with 47 East 91st Street has also shown that even good-neighbour designs can be radical. Architects take note: When designs are thwarted, sometimes the community, not the client, is to blame, says **Aimee Molloy.**

Cary Tamarkin, 140 Perry Street, New York, 1996

Opposite
The renovation of a 1909 stable building into eight 'raw' loft apartments was Tamarkin's first project as a developer.

Above
On completion of the project in 1996, Tamarkin decided to offer raw interior spaces on the market. The move allowed buyers to customise their interiors at a time when the New York real-estate market was only beginning to rebound from the recession of the early 1990s.

On the corner of New York's 91st Street and Madison Avenue, an apartment building rises. Housing seven apartments ranging in price from $5 million to $15 million, the 10-storey tower sits above an existing bank branch and is the first new residential building to be erected in the Carnegie Hill Historic District since 1950. As one might expect from Carnegie Hill, the upscale Manhattan neighbourhood that sits astride Museum Mile and Central Park, the tale of this tower is replete with all the trappings of a Hollywood screenplay. It has wealthy women arguing about architecture against an ambitious developer. There are lawyers and lawsuits and back-room dealings. And Woody Allen.

Meanwhile, in a loft space downtown, Cary Tamarkin is giving a quick tour of his office. Despite the 45-year-old's usually abrupt manner, he is eager to spend time explaining some of his favourite past projects: a conservatory and several outbuildings on a 10,000-acre Virginia ranch; a gate designed for an entrance on Quincy Street, in a choice section of Cambridge, Massachusetts; and sketches of picture frames and lighting fixtures, of which he seems particularly proud.

Tamarkin is a designer – of everything from lamps to apartment towers. 'I'm a talented artist and I work harder than probably anyone else,' he opines. But Tamarkin doesn't inhabit just a single identity. Tim Techler, his longtime friend, says: 'I think the most interesting thing about Cary is his hat rack.' He is speaking metaphorically of the many hats Tamarkin is known to wear: he is a musician, playing bluegrass guitar in the evening and until recently performing in care homes for the elderly and schools around the city. And he is the father of two young children. Of course, there are some overarching themes: 'I'm also a control freak,' he says, 'and hard to work with. Sometimes,' he shrugs, 'I steamroll people.'

Steamroll, indeed. Despite his odd collection of career artefacts and multifaceted resumé, Tamarkin is also a consummate businessman. He is the developer of the condominium 47 East 91st Street.

From the age of 12, Tamarkin knew that making money was as important to him as making great art. The two aren't easily reconciled, however, and Tamarkin was to struggle with this reality throughout his early career as an architect. Ultimately, his hunger for money led him to push architecture aside.

Tamarkin studied at the Harvard Design School and quickly showed promise. By the time he turned 26, his designs were placing in international competitions, including a

second-place entry with Tim Techler for a $52 million city hall and civic centre in Escondido, California. At 27, he sat at the helm of a firm he began with Techler. Two years later, he had forged a partnership with product designer George Kovacs and was managing a team of designers. For each design sold, Tamarkin kept half the profit.

Whilst developing an impressive portfolio of commissions and gaining a reputation as one of architecture's up-and-comers, Tamarkin was never content with the money he was making. 'I appreciated that my life had been devoted to making art,' he remembers, 'but I was walking around all day thinking about the fact that I'm not making money. There was no way I was going to spend my life as a starving artist. In one day, it all came to a head. That was the day I made four of the most important decisions of my life: to quit therapy, propose to my girlfriend, quit my job and abandon architecture as a career.'

Once the decision was made, he toyed with a host of new career possibilities, eventually settling on real-estate development, believing it presented a lucrative opportunity. 'I had no idea what I was doing when I chose real-estate development,' he says. 'When I told my wife, one of the first things she said was, "Do you

Tamarkin Techler Group,
Kluge Conservatory, Virginia,
1989

Below
Tamarkin was inspired by Jefferson's nearby Monticello home and the architecture of the surrounding Virginia countryside for this project. In his early career as an architect, he counted Arquitectonica and Robert A M Stern among his role models. The choice of materials and styling at Kluge reflects these influences.

Cary Tamarkin, 495 West Street, New York, 2001

Left
Tamarkin completed the first newly constructed loft building in New York's far West Village on an abandoned plot overlooking the Hudson River. The exterior of the building features alternating bands of corbelled light and dark brick combined with steel ribbon windows, making it highly compatible with its industrial-era neighbours, while its minimalist geometries and monumentality signify that it is a new modern addition to the Hudson River waterfront.

Below and bottom
The interior raw space reveals the powerful concrete superstructure of the building.

Cary Tamarkin, 206 West
17th Street, New York, 2002

Above
A conversion of a 12-storey
warehouse that was once
occupied by department store
Barney's. It now comprises 11
6,000-square-foot residential
lofts. The design reflects many
elements of Tamarkin's
previous projects, such as
steel-awning windows and
exposed-steel radiators.

Opposite
Like most of Tamarkin's
projects, the apartments at
206 West 17th Street were
conceived as raw loft space.
Their selling price per square
foot was among the highest
on the market at the time.

Tamarkin completely
renovated the interiors,
adding working
fireplaces and lifts
with 3,500-pound
capacity, but strove
to maintain as much
of the original detail
as possible, including
the original concrete
floors. He also
designed each as raw
loft space, lending
momentum to a real-
estate trend that
continues today.

really think you're tough enough?" She wasn't trying
to be mean but, come on, I was an architect.'

The next several years were to lead Tamarkin into
the dizzying new world of pro formas, negotiations,
delivery schedules and unruly neighbours. Starting out
with almost no knowledge of the New York City market,
he developed three luxury apartment buildings within
six years, each with financing from Oaktree Real Estate
Management in Los Angeles.

Of his first three projects, two were renovations of
existing buildings: a 1909 stable in the West Village and
the former warehouse of department store Barney's
New York. He completely renovated the interiors, adding
working fireplaces and lifts with 3,500-pound capacity,
but strove to maintain as much of the original detail as
possible, including the original concrete floors. He also
designed each as raw loft space, lending momentum
to a real-estate trend that continues today.

Tamarkin's one new construction project, an 11-
storey building overlooking the Hudson River, was
awarded a Design Award from the American Institute
of Architects. It is an elegant building of corbelled
buff-and-brown brick, reminiscent of the factories
that once surrounded the waterfront, but which resorts
more to modern geometries and large swaths of
glazing than it does historicist ornamentation.

Tamarkin, the controlling developer, managed
each aspect of these deals himself, from appeasing
neighbours unhappy with construction schedules to
keeping track of every dollar spent. But throughout
it all he proved unable to truly retire his architect
hat, serving as the architect of record for each of
his three buildings. He focused on the design as
much as the business side, something not always in
agreement. 'I knew that I couldn't tell my investors
what I was spending on design details and materials
– things like real steel window casings,' he recalls.
'But I had to be proud of the design if I was going
to be proud of the project.'

In turn, Tamarkin found the perfect investor in
Oaktree Financial. According to him, Oaktree did not
support his projects because they believed in good
design. 'Their only concern is making money,' he
says. 'And that was always at the forefront of my
mind.' But he knew that good design would mean that
the apartments would fetch higher prices, and thus a
higher return. 'I knew I had a limited market, because
most people wouldn't even care about the design
details these places offered,' he says. 'But I also knew
they'd sell easily, because they were so beautiful.'
And he was right. The apartments in his first two
buildings sold for a higher per-square-foot price
than anything on the market at the time, and
attracted buyers including Harrison Ford and Meryl
Streep. Oaktree made its return on investment and
Tamarkin became a millionaire.

Despite the ultimate success of these projects, Tamarkin recalls that: 'It was confusing. I was managing the business side of everything but also winning architecture awards. I never really knew how to describe myself. At parties I'd introduce myself as a developer but my wife was always correcting me, saying I was an architect.'

At a small bank building in Carnegie Hill, he was about to truly learn the largest difference between being an architect and becoming a developer: 'Everyone loves architects,' he says, 'and everyone hates developers.'

In New York, new development is rarely welcomed by the surrounding community. Tamarkin had faced modest opposition during his past development projects, but it was nothing compared to what he was about to confront in Carnegie Hill. The area is among the city's most exclusive, complete with tree-lined streets of multimillion-dollar brownstones, celebrity residents and the best private schools in the city. It is also one of the city's designated Historic Districts and any development is closely monitored to ensure it is in keeping with the historical context of the neighbourhood. Any new construction requires the approval of the Landmarks Commission, which has jurisdiction over the Historic Districts.

Tamarkin and Company purchased the air rights from the bank and set to work designing a 17-storey luxury apartment building to sit atop the bank. But local resident Carol McFadden, who had recently sold her townhouse at 92nd Street to Woody Allen, believed a 17-storey tower would dramatically alter the character of the neighbourhood. She set out to organise the residents of Carnegie Hill.

'I got a call from Carol, who had placed petitions in everyone's lobbies,' remembers Jane Pashall, who lives in the area with her husband David, a prominent

Cary Tamarkin, 47 East 91st Street, New York, completion due June 2004

Above
After its redesign as a 10-storey tower, as approved by the New York City Landmarks Commission, Tamarkin's latest and most controversial project isn't necessarily ruffling feathers because of its design. Indeed, the building marries classical proportions with an Art-Deco-style mullion pattern on its windows, two of the Carnegie Hill Historic District's favourite styles. Meanwhile, its inset corner window moves the design towards modernity by providing visual lightness to the building – and exposes the curtain walls for what they are.

attorney. 'I knew that I wanted to help. A tower would devastate Carnegie Hill.' The next day, Pashall had a card table set up across from the bank, distributing information about what was to become of the neighbourhood should Tamarkin have his way.

Within a few months, CitiNeighbors was formed. Its mission was to prevent a 'too-tall' building from being erected (the definition of which, however, was always a bit murky), and its membership list read like a Hollywood register: Woody Allen, Kevin Klein, Bette Midler and Paul Newman all participated in actions to oppose the building. Hearings before the Landmarks Commission became a media circus, starring Woody Allen quipping about architecture, historic integrity and the potential loss of his most revered movie set.

'It was such a terrible time,' Tamarkin recalls. 'I felt like I was being strung up by my toenails.' His 17-storey design was denied by the Landmarks Commission, which led him to do something entirely against his character – bring on a team of people to help, including architects to design the building. He found Charles Platt, of Platt Byard Dovell (PBD), who had recently published a book on new construction in historic districts and is the chair of the Historic Preservation programme at Columbia University – not to mention a Carnegie Hill resident.

'The opposition we faced with this building was nothing I would have ever anticipated,' remembers Platt. 'It was the biggest enemy to ever come to Carnegie Hill.'

Bill Coleman, Tamarkin's development partner who worked extensively on this project and who is also a resident of Carnegie Hill, says members of the opposition group have harassed him continuously over the last several months. 'I've had people calling me at 2 am at home,' he says. 'Recently some woman on the street I've never seen before starts yelling "Shame on you! Shame on you! This is war!"'

Not that Tamarkin relinquished control to PBD. He made important decisions, such as reducing the number of storeys, and by how many. In fact, Landmarks Commissioner Jennifer Raab would not allow Tamarkin to proceed without the collaboration. 'She told me that there was no way that I was going to stand in front of them worrying about the number of bathrooms I could stuff in there when she's trying to talk about architecture,' he explains. He also considered trying to use architecture's 'international stars' but decided against it, thinking he'd be too intimidated working with them and wouldn't be able to have as much input into the design as he could with PBD (a firm he claims to respect, and which was not simply a front for his own design work).

A design was approved after two failed proposals and 21 months of bickering. The final building sits at 10 storeys, seven less than the original proposal.

It's not easy to say who won the war. 'When I talk to the neighbours,' Tamarkin says, 'I tell them they won because they prevented a 17-storey building from being built. But really I think that I won. I have a great building which, although it's not exactly the design I would have done, works as a piece of architecture and a development deal.'

The neighbours, however, are anything but happy. CitiNeighbors has filed a lawsuit against Tamarkin and Co, the Landmarks Commission and Oaktree Financial Group. A decision is currently pending. Should CitiNeighbors win, Tamarkin may be required to take down any portion of the building deemed illegal. And all of this has come at a tremendous expense to both parties. During the months of

working for approval from the Landmarks Commission, Tamarkin had $10 million in financing accruing interest. CitiNeighbors, work for which is being fully funded by local residents, has footed all of the legal bills. 'I'm not comfortable saying how much has been spent,' says David Pashall, 'but it's a substantial amount, and will continue to be substantial until this issue is resolved.'

'This whole thing was surreal,' Tamarkin says of the battle. 'I'm suddenly this terrible enemy. I'm fighting with Woody Allen. This project is all over the papers and I've got lawyers and PR people and a whole contingent of people following me around. All of a sudden, I felt like a real New York City developer, and that felt great.'

Perhaps, in the end, this will suspend his confusion of how to introduce himself at parties. But it's more likely that Cary Tamarkin will continue to think up new hats to wear, constantly reinventing himself. 'Where do I think I'll end up?' he considers. 'Part of me thinks I'll become a big New York City developer, building hotels and skyscrapers. The other part of me thinks I'll quit everything and become a painter. I have this attic in my townhouse,' he muses. As it turns out, Tamarkin – architect, developer, musician, steamroller, father – has already begun designing the studio. ᴅ

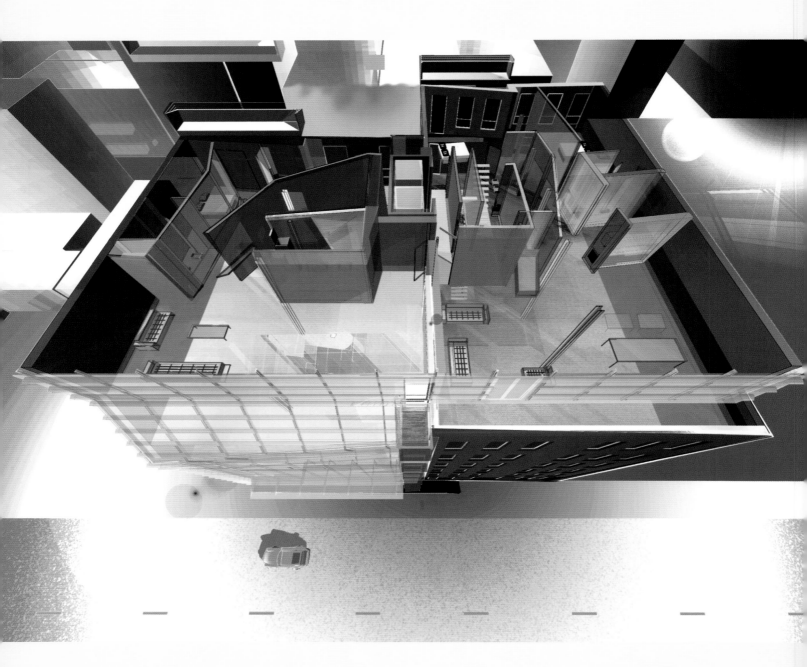

When Jonathon Carroll debuted as a property developer he opted for the unexpected. As he was transplanted from London to New York, he hired Archi-Tectonics' Winka Dubbeldam to design a condominium building that's not for the faint-of-heart marketer. In a keen interpretation of the New York City building code, Dubbeldam juxtaposed provocative contemporary architecture with the historic urban fabric. **David B Sokol** discovers why Carroll allowed such design freedom and what he's learnt for the next time around.

Jonathon Carroll is a wunderkind. A career in finance took the twenty-something Birmingham native to Credit Suisse First Boston and Nomura International, and then afforded him retirement at the ripe old age of 33.

Wunderkinds, however, can't sit still. In 2000 Carroll moved to New York, into a cavernous Soho loft designed by Archi-Tectonics principal Winka Dubbeldam, completed in 1998. The loft, Dubbeldam says, 'presented the challenge of making 5,000 square feet comfortable for one person. Rather than the traditional separation into rooms, the space is divided into overlapping zones.' The loft's central nucleus is a concrete master-bathroom suite, wrapped around which is an undulating glass wall that creates and defines public and private zones within the apartment. Dubbeldam adds that Carroll's loft includes many elements that pivot, hinge and rotate in order to 'create different scenarios, different levels of privacy and openness'. Thanks to Dubbeldam maintaining the loft's original sense of scale, the residence was also an exercise in reconceiving proportions, in everything from furniture to kitchens.

Brit in the Big City

Opposite
Archi-Tectonics, Greenwich Street project, SoHo, New York, 2003
While interior walls reference the angularity of the building's exterior, each of the Greenwich Street project's 22 units is ostensibly conceived as an open-plan loft residence.

Above
Archi-Tectonics, SoHo loft designed for Jonathon Carroll, New York, 1997
The glazed screen in the 5,000-foot loft wraps around a central bathroom core to define the public and private zones within the space. Because this strategy does not sacrifice the loft's sense of magnitude and openness, Dubbeldam carefully chose larger-scale furnishings.

Carroll had settled in New York not to revel in his new home but to do business. By 2000 he had launched his property development company Take One LLC with the purchase of a six-storey warehouse as well as a single-storey garage just south of Soho. The goal: rehabilitate the 1908 warehouse, demolish the garage and build in its place an architecturally distinctive structure, and then connect both historic and contemporary buildings as one 22-unit condominium.

Dubbeldam was chosen for the job because of the history architect and client shared. Carroll recalls: 'Winka was involved in that bridge period between working on my apartment and me saying to her, "By the way, I'm seriously thinking about switching careers and getting involved in development in New York," and I think she saw an opportunity to collaborate. She worked with me to find the site. We spent a long time walking around, looking around. Winka had a greater insight into the things that I wanted to see, than if we hadn't met before.'

Dubbeldam tells it a little differently: 'Aren't you interested in doing a building? Isn't it better than stocks and bonds?' she remembers jokingly saying to Carroll. But regardless of exactly who initiated Carroll's change of career, the pair began their search for sites.

At 497 Greenwich Street, Dubbeldam found her canvas. She says that Archi-Tectonics 'has been very lucky with its clientele in general,' and with Carroll she was given an almost completely free rein in the design. ('The first constraint was that we were going to keep the old building, and I think that in itself is a very powerful parameter to apply,' Carroll explains, adding, 'There were also building regulation restraints, such as the setback. The building is 90 per cent driven by these two constraints.')

The consequent design is an innovative juxtaposition of old and new structure, and of New York City setback requirements. The new building has a complicated folded-glass facade that recedes as it travels upwards, to meet the setback requirement. Another visual accomplishment is that its uppermost five storeys appear to cantilever over its warehouse neighbour, in fact sitting above it and sharing a vertical circulation core. The marriage of different architectures is a meditation on memory and change and redefines the possibilities of parabuildings.

Archi-Tectonics, Greenwich Street project, SoHo, New York, 2003

Right
Detail of the intricate glass curtain wall.

Below
Exploded section clearly showing one of the design's defining characteristics – its folded-glass curtain wall.

Opposite
Aerial renderings.

'Developers are very suspicious of architects because they think they're artists who just want to create something to put their name on. And likewise, I think architects think that developers have no interest in design architecture, and are just out there to make a quick buck. I think that too many developers place so many restrictions that an architect feels less like an architect and more like a project manager. But there is a middle ground.'

A set of balconies is also placed between the two buildings. This so-called 'crease' animates a streetscape already enlivened by the goings-on behind the modern addition's glass front. It is one element that leads Dubbeldam to claim, 'Greenwich was an urban study, really'.

Not that it was easy to turn this urban study into material reality. Financing the $38 million project was perhaps the biggest hurdle. On the one hand, 'because my background is financial and I can bore you to death stress-testing spreadsheets,' says Carroll, 'even with fairly aggressive additional costs I was fairly confident that I could make it work.'

On the other, 'I was aware from day one that it was going to be tough for me,' and Carroll paid for the first nine months of work (which comprised obtaining the variance to build anew on the garage's plot and finishing the design) out of his own pocket before presenting a comprehensive financial package to any bank. Still, the initial response was not optimistic. 'They told me how wonderful the project was, but they had a policy of not making loans to first-time developers, irrespective of the project, irrespective of the amount of equity put into the project. It was just a rule they could not break. At one point I couldn't believe this was happening.

'It was a very different meeting with First Bank & Trust of Illinois,' however. 'They are a privately owned bank, and their decision-making processes are what you might call streamlined. So rather than have a layering of bureaucracy, I actually met the guy who was the CEO of the bank, on site. They offered to finance pretty much that day, on the spot. And I moved forward with them.'

The Greenwich Street project was completed in the autumn of 2003. Carroll has marketed the fraternal twins with Dubbeldam's help. 'I think originally we were thinking that the marketing would be consistent with the style theme of the building,' Carroll says. 'Therefore it was important to me that Winka had some input in that creative process early on, which she did. I think it would have been a negative if there was a disjoint between the building and the whole marketing seemed to have come from somewhere else, so I think it's important to have elements coming through in the marketing side of it.' Even beyond marketing architecture, Carroll believes that architects 'should be prepared to cross the lines a little bit and add their expertise wherever they can'.

And the reason why architects should work beyond their contractual scope? To aid in precluding the bad blood that seems to develop between architects and property developers. 'I feel very strongly about that,' Carroll starts. He describes the legendary animosity: 'Developers are very suspicious of architects because they think they're artists who just want to create

**Archi-Tectonics, Greenwich
Street project, SoHo,
New York, 2003**

Opposite
The Greenwich Street project's
ground floor includes a gallery
space in addition to common
areas.

Above
Completed facade. Balconies
at the far end serve as an
intersection, or 'crease',
between new architecture and
a 1908 warehouse.

something to put their name on. And likewise, I think architects think that developers have no interest in design architecture, and are just out there to make a quick buck. I think that too many developers place so many restrictions that an architect feels less like an architect and more like a project manager. But there is a middle ground.'

Another hint for improving architect–client relations is archispeak, or lack thereof. 'Key to any project is being able to communicate effectively with each other. Architects articulate some things that the developer or the contractor thinks is a different language.'

With some lessons learnt and a potential icon in his pocket, Carroll plans to take a rest before starting on another project. When he does, though, he plans to follow a similar route

of commissioning a progressive design from an up-and-coming architect. While Carroll admits that he is developing a niche product, he says that 'the interest in talking to quote-unquote "non-celebrity" architects is that when you start you have much less of an idea of where you're going. For me, that's part of the exciting process.

'And besides,' he adds, 'the premium value of being in, say, a Meier building versus that other building will go down as it becomes common.'

So finding that next architect 'is the top of my to-do list. For me that's the only reason I want to be more known, because that's the way of accessing new people, new minds. I think it will probably be more difficult than you'd imagine. There are an awful lot of architects out there, and you end up working with an architect for three years, so there are a lot of factors you have to consider.' ◬

Risky

In the realm of speculative office-building, breaking aesthetic convention is usually met with apprehension or avoided at all costs. Phoenix architect **Eddie Jones** explains how he learnt the hard way. His studio's NAI Horizon Corporate Office Building, completed in

Business

January 2000, is a diaphanous volume that is admirably green in its design — and was built for only $88 per square foot. Here he tells of the client's initial scepticism, a Sonoran tradition and subverting a manufacturer's blacklist.

Why do office buildings in Manhattan have to look like buildings in Los Angeles? Why can downtown buildings located in Minneapolis appear in Dallas, Denver and Phoenix? I now know that developers, bankers, appraisers, estate agents and even urban planners have formulas based on market research which, when combined with the applicable zoning ordinances, are guaranteed to produce profits – and repetitive mediocrity.

Jones Studio, Inc's reputation for environmentally responsible building design apparently suggests that we are fiscally irresponsible. So a group of international investors were understandably sceptical about the decision to commission Jones Studio, Inc for the design of the NAI Horizon Corporate Office Building. Fortunately, Scott O'Conner convinced his partners to consider the corporate tagging possibilities of an architecture distinguished from similar building programmes.

The architects wanted an urban, desert building. The developer, on the other hand, wanted 'bottom line'. The time-tested challenge was to reconcile disparate goals. The architects began by acknowledging the validity of both points of view and quickly realised a common aspiration: architecture for the developer market.

Reconciling Wants

There is a Sonoran desert-dweller tradition of building passive solar-shading elements, called *ramada*, in which saguaro cactus ribs are laced between Palo Verde 'columns'. In a contemporary interpretation, the NAI Horizon building uses a sawdust-and-recycled-plastic-polymer composite extruded in 2x2-inch strips to produce a zero-maintenance shade screen that weathers with age.

This so-called solar filter spaces 1.5x1.5-inch lattice with 1.5-inch airspace between each member, which produces an average 45-degree cutoff and essentially shades 50 per cent of the entire exterior skin. A minimal steel-angle framework, suspended 5 feet from the building surface, supports the screen. In all, it allows natural daylight into the building without the resulting heat gain and thus reduces the need for electric lighting during the day. The use of high-efficiency heat pumps combined

Jones Studio, Inc, NAI Horizon Corporate Office Building, Phoenix, 2000

Previous spread
Locally known as the 'lobster trap', the Horizon building shades itself without sacrificing daylight.

Right
The two-by-two composite-wood sun filter is suspended 5 feet off the exterior walls.

Below
Evening hours produce a swap in lighting levels revealing a veiled transparency.

Opposite
Eastern philosophy suggests that a pattern cannot be appreciated until it is interrupted!

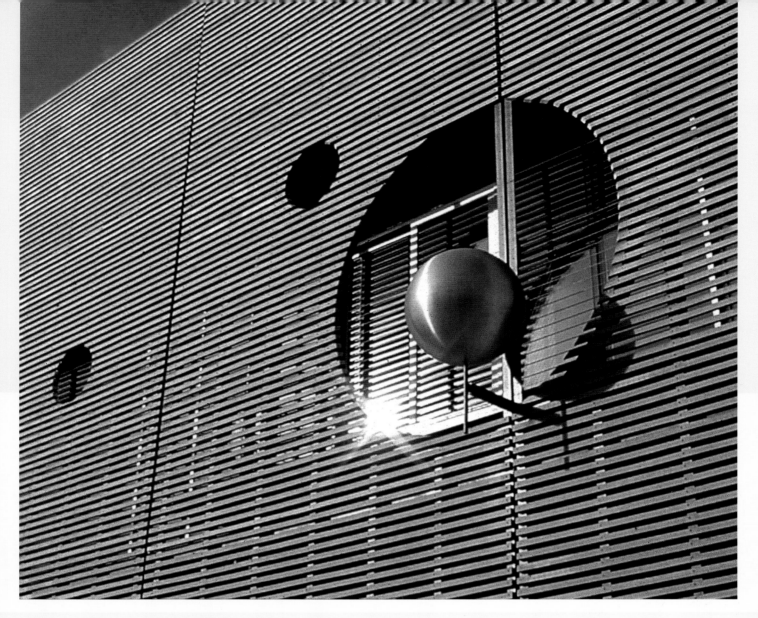

with total screen enclosure decreased HVAC tonnage by 20 per cent. Strategically positioned operable windows permitted natural ventilation, and rainwater harvesting fed concentrated points of indigenous landscaping.

Meanwhile, ratios for required parking and leasable square footage support functions to usable space, and current construction costs versus local leasing rates defined site-planning issues and structural/mechanical systems. A very simple post-and-beam steel structure and economical glazing system offset the cost of the building's lattice sun filter.

Unlike similar office buildings, this project open-mindedly explores many criteria, including climate, site, material efficiency and indoor air-pollution reduction without falling back on a predetermined style or image. It questions every line and component in order to make it more responsible and more efficient. Arbitrary stylistic choices were avoided and were replaced by a methodology of first reducing a particular idea, material or system to its bare essence, then designing it to serve two or more functions and finally discovering and closing its environmental 'loops' (from cradle to grave to cradle again) to minimise waste.

But I'll never forget the first time we presented the concept rendering for this building. The latticework was clearly articulated as a see-through layer. Despite congenial conversation, on Monday morning Mr O'Conner informed us that the investors hated it. Not only did they not 'get it', the commercial real-estate broker thought it was 'butt ugly'.

Bittersweet Resolutions

So we explored other possible solutions which might deliver similar results, but in evaluating materials, ease of constructibility, costs and daylight/heat-gain balance, nothing matched the efficiency of the composite section. We evaluated galvanised-metal furring channels as lattice. We tested the use of three-quarter-inch-round electrical conduit as a screen. We looked at fritted glass patterns. Each of the alternatives had advantages, but the costs were usually excessive.

Finally, with the co-operation of the general contractor and support of Scott O'Conner we began full-scale mock-ups using the composite material as horizontal two-by-twos and comparing it with 1x4- and 1x6-inch slanted louvre configurations. We invited the investors to the construction yard to view the experiment and, amazingly, they began to see the logic behind the idea.

We could now get to work, but then came what appeared to be an insurmountable problem. Whilst the original manufacturer of the composite sun-screen material had been very excited to see the product in a commercial sun-control application, once we were well into construction the manufacturing facility was sold and the new owner refused to sell us the material, deeming its use in the project as too risky.

We required 30,000 lineal feet of two-by-twos. We contacted other suppliers in other cities, but found they had all been alerted. So we conspired to purchase 10,000 lineal feet of 2x6-inch slats, which we had shipped to a Tucson contractor who

Above right
Natural daylight becomes manifest through its opposite – shadow.

Far right
The architects extended resource-efficient criteria to the design of the interior.

Right
Panel detailing allowed the sun screen to be economically prefabricated in the car park, later to be hoisted into position.

Opposite, top
Ramada is a traditional Papago Native American shade structure built with saguaro cactus ribs laid horizontally, supported by Palo Verde branches.

Opposite, bottom
Original coloured rendering by Eddie Jones.

then sold it back to us without mark-up. We then had it ripped into two-by-twos and delivered to the job site. One can only imagine the potential legal consequences.

Ironically, our best 'partner' was the leap-of-faith attitude shared by the owner and contractor. The architects found little support from city officials nor, more surprisingly, from material suppliers. The client wanted a building that would architecturally distinguish the company and set a new standard for energy-efficient speculative office-buildings. The challenge for the architects was to achieve these noble goals without exceeding the construction costs of more conventional spec buildings, and the project was therefore built for $88 per square foot!

Known locally as the 'lobster trap', the Horizon office building has been recognised through awards and by numerous publications. It was fully occupied within just four months and we still receive complimentary testimonials from the people who work there.

After a year of operation, Arizona State University environmental design students conducted an energy analysis on the Horizon building. Although the report confirmed our power-conservation projections, the students were able to show diagrammatically that significant improvement could be achieved by simply altering the direction of the sun-screen slats relative to solar exposure for each building elevation.

Nevertheless, the students' exercise gets to the heart of this story: validating architecture requires non-innovative cost analysis and financing. We had set out to prove that responsible, viable, site-appropriate design can be financed and developed for the open-minded investor. And for profit. ∆

Calibrating the Commercial Potential:

An Interview with John Ritblat

Founded in 1856, British Land is one of the oldest publicly listed property groups. Led by its chairman, John Ritblat, it has been the major player in British property development since the 1960s. **Jeremy Melvin** talked to Ritblat and his colleagues at British Land about the shifting commercial and construction climate, and how over the years it has informed their selection of architects and the way projects are run.

'We would love to work with Gehry or Herzog & de Meuron,' says John Ritblat, long-serving chairman and managing director of British Land, one of Britain's largest property companies. They are working with Norman Foster and Richard Rogers on large projects in the City of London. Experience built up over several decades has shown Ritblat and his colleagues how to get the most from architects of this calibre. Back in the 1960s it might have been enough for a developer to give a brief to Richard Seifert, the legendary commercial architect of postwar Britain, and not go back until the building was completed. Now, however, explains Ritblat, 'We wouldn't leave an architect to put anything up on their own; we insist on tight project management.'

'In fairness to today's architects,' adds Stephen Kalman, former director of development and still a consultant to the company, 'buildings were simpler in the 1960s. They're more complex now.' And while that complexity has taken the process of producing buildings some way out of architects' competence, they have compensated with designs that respond more positively to the combination of environmental, commercial and aesthetic factors which contribute to successful development.

It was not until the 1980s that there were 'the beginnings of the first modern buildings', contends Ritblat. From 1945 until then the construction industry was dominated by the myth of prefabrication and government-inspired rationing of land and building materials. The economic strictures of the Second World War and their aftermath cast a long shadow: rationing of construction materials did not end until 1951 and rationing of building land, by

some accounts, continues today through the planning system. Recalling the 'Brown Ban', an attempt in the 1960s by the then Labour Chancellor of the Exchequer George Brown to prohibit office building except in selected areas like Croydon, where no one wanted to go, evinces a laugh from Ritblat and his cohorts: 'We made a fortune,' he remembers, because anyone with a building in a popular location had a monopoly and could charge more or less what they liked. Similarly Office Development Permits and the Development Land Tax, an attempt to tax the value that accrues to a planning consent, did little for public finances and less for the quality of the built environment.

Restricted in land and materials, the construction industry only had prewar designs and techniques of prefabrication to meet postwar expansion. Everything, even the fortunes of political parties, was driven by a need to build cheaply and fast. Limitations on the amount of steel available for construction meant that a great skill in steel construction – as shown in the prewar phases of Plantation House in the City – was squandered and the industry driven to use concrete with no expertise in its use or understanding of how it would age. The consequence was that 'shops looked like garages and offices looked like boxes and were not much higher,' says Ritblat. Although in 1951 the 'Festival of Britain changed a little, it was the first decent postwar architecture', but the scope for commercial development was severely curtailed by fragmented ownership of land and 'very difficult regulations'.

At the time, remembers Ritblat, 'architects were not employed for their stylistic attributes but to maximise planning consents'. Seifert's great skill, and attractiveness to a generation of developers, was that he could 'exploit inexpert planners'. After the Second World War, demand for office space, when copying machines and other equipment took up a great deal

of space, was so huge and supply so limited that any building 'let immediately and there was no incentive for quality'. Even as restrictions began to lighten and design acquired more scope, opportunities were wasted. What Ritblat calls 'Postmodern architects', like William Holford and Frederick Gibberd, designed 'absolutely ghastly [buildings], with no sense of how to cope with wind'. The blame for postwar desecration lies, he believes, first with planners and then developers, 'aided and abetted by architects'. With 'no complete plan for London' piecemeal regulations and the capriciousness of borough planning officers made an almost impossible framework against which to develop decent environments.

Amid the general mess there were a few brighter spots. Denys Lasdun brought 'a finer sense of appropriateness'. John Summerson engendered an appreciation of London's inherent urban qualities. Louis de Soissons designed good buildings though in a prewar mode, and Sydney Kaye, designer of the Hilton Hotel on Park Lane and the Euston Centre, 'was good at towers'. But these qualities arose as often as not because the basic designs were enormously overspecified, and allowed change, as it were by accident, rather than because of any particular foresight on the part of the architects. Ritblat remembers one example well: Plantation House, built partly prewar and finished after 1945 to the original design which, aided by Bryan Avery's 'brilliant' refurbishment of the common parts and with British Land's strategy of short leases and providing services, yielded up to £15 million

a year. But even that was dwarfed by the eventual redevelopment of the site, which brought about a massive 'uplift in space'. A less happy example was Lambeth Bridge House, designed and built on either side of the war and obsolete before it was completed. However, it took until the end of the 1990s before it was replaced – with EPR's Parliament View apartments for which British Land obtained planning consent.

For a generation after the war a limited supply of land, buildings, building materials and imaginative design meant that profit lay in holding property only at certain key moments in the development cycle, such as obtaining an upgraded planning consent. As these constituents have altered, the balance has swung to assembling large areas and improving them over the long term. During our conversation, Ritblat and his present director of development, Nigel Webb, and head of planning and environment, Adrian Penfold, as well as the veteran Stephen Kalman who joined British Land in 1972, slowly unfolded the series of steps by which maximising value has become a more sophisticated cocktail of design, construction management, and environmental and social initiatives than in the days when exploiting loopholes in legislation sufficed.

Ritblat offers little about his developments of the 1960s and 1970s, perhaps because at that time the interaction of market and political forces meant that trading or holding, rather than developing property, were more attractive, though he becomes enthusiastic about British Land's developments from the 1980s onwards. It is perhaps no coincidence that his change of attitude coincides with a political watershed. Once the most overt political interference in land and property values had ended by the mid-1970s, demand for office space became 'more or less sensible, though cyclical', providing more incentive and a more stable background for development.

In the City of London at least the cycle swung upwards in the early 1980s and the best buildings from that date are the earliest, which remain habitable without major refurbishment. At the front of the line was No 1 Finsbury Avenue designed by Arup Associates' Peter Foggo in 1984, and credited to Stuart Lipton as developer. Ritblat's British Land arranged the financing, which began a long involvement with the area, culminating in British Land's ownership of the whole of Broadgate, including an ongoing £40 million improvement programme for the public areas there, and a £50 million, 160,000-square-foot new building by Skidmore, Owings & Merrill (SOM) at 10 Exchange Square, due for completion in the second quarter of 2004.

An example of these trends is the Euston Centre, an unlovely composition of slabs and towers built as a joint venture between Joe Levy's Stock Conversion and Wimpey to designs by Sydney Kaye Firmin. In 1985 British Land bought Wimpey's half and has gradually acquired further parcels, taking its ownership to over 10 acres, as well as entering into an agreement with the Crown which owns the western end of the site. This gives British Land control of the entire 15-acre urban block. With Euston, King's Cross and Baker Street all in close proximity, and an imminent uplift when St Pancras becomes an international terminal, the site's transport links offered enormous potential but required a balance of architecture, forms of tenure and amenities to exploit it.

Opportunities for redevelopment arose as the leases fell in. The first major project was a reconstruction and widening of 338 Euston Road, a tower at the western end by architects Sheppard Robson, and the first newbuild was No 1 Triton Square, a large rectangular building that forms one side of a new pedestrianised public space. Designed by James Burland, then of Arup Associates, it introduced the first major new amenity to the site, the Broadgate Club by Allford Hall Monaghan Morris. At that stage, before critical mass was achieved, British Land built and managed the facility itself, though it has now been taken on by Holmes Place.

Other amenities included a crèche and new shops like Sainsbury's Local and Pret a Manger in the reconstruction podium to the Euston Tower.

And further developments on the site followed, with Sheppard Robson designing new buildings at 350 Euston Road and 2/3 Triton Square. Terry Farrell is master-planning the rest of the site as well as designing the next building, and other architects will also be appointed, probably after an informal competition.

Regent's Place, as the development is now known, demonstrates several attributes of British Land's development strategy, and the role of architecture within it. It is a large site with good communications and infrastructure – 'We wouldn't look at anything without the right infrastructure,' stresses Ritblat – and no architecture could compensate for poor communications. Secondly, as British Land has developed it, it contains a mix of facilities with varying degrees of public access, from an open square through a balance of retail offerings to the health club, all interacting to create a skein of attractions to the site in addition to the quality of office space. Obviously such a balance needs a site of some size, something British Land realised long before Broadgate was conceived. Ritblat refers to Setanta, a large development and the first 'fully equipped' modern offices in Dublin of the early 1970s, where art and amenities were mixed to great effect.

Underpinning the trend towards larger-scale developments is the shift in planning skills from the public to private sectors. Where once local authorities,

with fully resourced planning departments and even an in-house architects team, expected to undertake what master-planning there was, Adrian Penfold points out that responsibility, now far more technically sophisticated, falls to the private sector. And as planning becomes more sophisticated and responsive it branches into the whole area of social responsibility, another area that once would have fallen entirely into the purlieu of public bodies. British Land is 'looking to do more work' in Penfold's words, 'to explore the approach to key environmental issues', especially along its supply chains, and expects to have 'two-way discussions' with architects and other professional consultants.

Improving the experience of visiting or using its developments is a central plank of British Land's strategy. This starts with making buildings legible and giving them identity, as Bryan Avery brought coherence to the labyrinthine communal spaces in the old Plantation House. But it also comes through the dimension that art can bring to public areas. The improvements to Broadgate will maximise the setting of Richard Serra's giant steel sculpture there, while special commissions at Regent's Place include a spectacularly large piece by Michael Craig-Martin. Other leading British artists to be involved include Langlands and Bell, Antony Gormley, Liam Gillick, Sarah Morris and Fiona Rae. This echoes the roster of art from a different generation in the firm's headquarters: Pasmores line the entrance hall and Hepworths flank the main staircase.

Using different architects and giving them buildings of different shapes and heights to design or refurbish adds further to the variety on offer, and consequently the way British Land selects architects is revealing. Less obviously a collector of 'starchitects' than Stanhope, the company often uses some form of beauty parade, which was how it selected Terry Farrell, though long an admirer of his work. But as Kalman confirms, there is quite a lot of intuition in deciding which architect is most appropriate for a given job, a point Ritblat makes explicit: 'We don't think each architect is suitable for every job.' Arup Associates is a firm whose name crops up several times, over the redevelopment of the Plantation House site where Arup's did a brilliant design for a 23- to 26-storey tower. 'And we almost managed it: we should have done a tower there,' muses Ritblat. But that was before Foster and Swiss Re forced the City to rethink its policy towards tall buildings. This change has created another opportunity for a tower at 122 Leadenhall Street. Being directly opposite, and almost a homage to, the Lloyds Building, 'Rogers was the only architect' considered. After its airings at last year's Venice Biennale and this year's Royal Academy Sky High show, it became clear that 'everyone loves the design,' enthuses Ritblat. Meanwhile, Foster has been instructed for a million-square-footer round the corner on the site of the old Lloyds headquarters, which has planning consent subject to Section 106 agreements.

Ritblat regrets not having worked with Philip Johnson in the past, but what of the future? There's nothing – as yet – with Gehry or Herzog & de Meuron, though he is talking to Chris Wilkinson, he adds. 'It might be Hopkins or Grimshaw – they've all got a role' – a role that fits into a more flexible and sophisticated context than the days when all one needed for a quick fortune was to leave it to Colonel Seifert. △

Reconciling the Irreconcilable?
The Architecture of
Ken Yeang

Born into a family involved in property development in Penang, Malaysia, Ken Yeang's work seeks to reconcile the seemingly irreconcilable, as he pursues ecologically sensitive design solutions worldwide, often in a commercially competitive construction environment. **Helen Castle** found out from Yeang just what an important part sound costings and client credibility play in his practice and how they can effectively aid the advancement of a progressive architectural agenda.

Progressing Progressive Architecture

Ken Yeang is a progressive architect in the most proactive as well as creative sense of the word. Ever since he published his first article on the 'Bases for Ecosystem Design' in *Architectural Design* as a research student at Cambridge at the tender age of 24, he has been progressing ecological design and his conception of it.[1] He has achieved this through constant research, publication and international lecturing. The amount of global travel he undertakes in a year is prodigious: on the day of our interview we meet at his hotel in London for an hour, as a stopgap for Yeang who has come over to Bristol from Kuala Lumpur for the day.

The architecture Yeang has designed and produced with Hamzah & Yeang from his office in Kuala Lumpur can be regarded as a consolidation and development of his 1981 Cambridge PhD dissertation on the incorporation of ecological considerations in architectural design and planning.[2] As Leon van Schaik has pointed out, this transposition of research into architecture can be seen to most dramatic effect in the way Yeang translated his later 1986 study into the naturally ventilated and shaded architecture of Kuala Lumpur, 'The Tropical Verandah City', into built form. Seemingly through no more than a sleight of hand or vertical subversion, the verandah city became Yeang's bioclimatic skyscraper.

Light-heartedly van Schaik evocatively imagines for us the Eureka effect of Yeang trumping Alvin Boyarsky or another of his Architectural Association contemporaries, sneering at his provincial verandah designs, by creating his own Manhattan towers and 'setting his street section [of the verandah city] on end'.[3] This simple rotation from low-rise vernacular to high-rise verdant metropolis may or may not have been the result of a single impulse, but Yeang has relentlessly pursued it in his written and built work until it has become an established typology.

Van Schaik outlines three stages of research, design and development Yeang has undertaken in his office with the bioclimatic skyscraper: the first series, between 1975 and 1988, largely consisted of primary investigations that tested out a single component of the bioclimatic ideal; in the second series, from 1989 to 1993, completed prototypes emerged and the bioclimatic concept was developed further; and the final series of 1994 to 1996 resulted in technical refinement to the prototypes and the formal expression of the idea.[4] The speed of current practice necessitates that Yeang learns effectively on the hop, directly from what he designs and constructs, improving on each project in front of him. Now globally renowned for his verdant vision of streets in the sky, overflowing with foliage from every available balcony or opening, Yeang continues to push forward and surprise. In the last few years he has rotated 90 degrees again, returning to the horizontal, with his experiments with the groundscraper or subscraper.[5] Low- and medium-rise buildings are for Yeang a primary investigation into counteracting the ecological impact of a greater horizontal mass or footprint. This is not only a matter of limitation, guarding against the disruption of virgin topsoil in greenfield sites, and ensuring the maintenance of 'linked or continuously vegetated planting zones as "ecological corridors"' in master plans, but also poses the potential for creating new ecological habitats. This is achieved through the 'greening' of the realised built form with vertical and horizontal landscapes, as the large roof surfaces become important sites for vegetation.[6]

Reconciling the Irresistible Drives of Economic Growth

What makes Kenneth Yeang's position so unique is his remarkable 'reconciliation of opposites'.[7] As van Schaik has highlighted in his essay 'Simultaneity' in *Ecocells*: 'Only one architect has made it his major project to attempt to reconcile the irresistible drives of "economic growth" … When developers rushed headlong into Manhattan mode, Yeang attempted to subvert their flight from the horizontal into bioclimatically designed eco-towers. He used his science to co-opt the vertical into the same daydream of the healthy social organism of the prosperous town.'

Yeang was brought up in a Modernist villa in Penang, Malaysia, designed by Svenson Van Sitterson, and his father was an active property speculator. It seems that the pragmatics of finance and construction were ingrained from the first, along with a bent for original thinking and a determination to progress the visionary.[8] As van Schaik explains: 'Like all of the contemporaries he lists, Yeang was already "seeking the difference" when he went to the Architectural Association School of Architecture in London. Like any successful speculator, he has going against the grain as second nature.'[9]

Yeang's decision to continue his studies at Cambridge, after aligning himself with Peter Cook and the Archigram group at the AA, was equally characteristic and independent minded. Setting out to fully research the ecological impact of the built environment, he sought

Previous page
Kenneth Yeang.

Opposite
Rendering of the New National
Library Building, Singapore.

Competition Client
The New National Library Building, Singapore (completion due December 2004)

Hamzah & Yeang won the competition for the New National Library Building, Singapore, in an international competition in October 1998, in which Yeang's entry was pitched against an impressive short list of candidates: Michael Graves, Mitchell Guirgola, Moshe Safdie and Nikken Sekkei. The opportunity to create a national and civic institution for Singapore distinguished it from other competitions for Yeang, and his response to the brief differentiated it from the world-class competition for the client. As Christopher Chia, chief executive of the National Library Board, explains: 'We were rather taken by the amount of thought and preparation put into Ken's design even during the earliest stages of the process. He had considered the architectural, cultural and physical environmental context for the building; and the result is anticipated to be one of Singapore's most endearing buildings for the coming decades.'[10]

Through the New National Library Building, Hamzah & Yeang is setting out to create a new aesthetic landmark and civic focus for Singapore. The exterior of the building will distinguish itself from its surroundings through its distinct assemblage of sun shades (6 metres deep in places), which confer it with a distinctly tropical character. The built form will essentially consist of two blocks separated by a naturally lit, semi-enclosed internal street, connected at the upper level by bridges. The larger block, overlooking the internal plaza, will contain the library collections, and the curved smaller block will contain the more bustling public activities such as exhibitions, multimedia events and lectures. Though functional requirements necessitate that the library is to be fully air-conditioned, passive mode strategies have been adopted (optimised daylight, good solar orientation and configuration, sun shading, natural ventilation, responsive facade design, appropriate building colour and use of landscaping), so that the energy embodiment costs and the environmental impact of the building are substantially lower than the typical office building.

'through his doctorate the proper tools for achieving their [Archigram's] dreams of moving, responsive and self-mending cities.'[11]

Just as Yeang has carved out an unprecedented role for himself, in both southeast Asia and the rest of the world, as a 'green' architect working with the skyscraper (a type that since its very genesis in Chicago and Manhattan has come to epitomise commerce and speculative development), Hamzah & Yeang has sought its own way financially. As Yeang explained to me: 'We learnt to control costs and how to do the financials the hard way by working with cost-conscious developers in our early years, from about 30 years ago. We became expert in cost control and in value engineering and this led to repeat work.'[12]

Yeang describes the process: 'We usually do the financials for the client from day one or, if not, we usually help him establish his budget for the project. In doing this it gives us greater control of the design as it gives us an idea of how much contingency sums and leeway we can expend to provide more creative and novel solutions. Most, if not all clients are very particular about how the architect manages his money, and if we show careful concern from day one it builds confidence.'[13]

For Yeang, the client provides the axis for good architectural collaboration and thus high-quality work. A current situation of distrust has arisen in construction only as a result of the loss of the architect's position as the client's friend, and it is important to rectify this. Often the architect is perceived to have an adversary role, in which he or she has differing or even opposing aims to the client. At the crux of this is the relegation of cost control to project managers and quantity surveyors, which expresses an abdication of financial responsibility but also a loss of desire to look after the client's best interests.[14] Thus in every case Hamzah & Yeang is careful to work 'backwards by designing from the financials or from the client's budget. The figures then provide us with a basis for creative conceptualisation and we make sure that this does not inhibit novel solutions in any way.'[15]

So the door is left open to talking to the client about alternative solutions if the budget is prohibitive, but this is very different from many architects whose solutions are often the upshot of a compromised concept, which has been pared back and pared back from their own ideal through financial imperatives. For Yeang, the time spent on briefing and understanding the client's needs thus becomes formative. Rather than presenting a set of restrictions, the brief should be the springboard

Client Acquiring a Signature Building
Palomas II Tower, Mexico City
(commencement of design April 2003)

This project for an apartment block in a wealthy area of Mexico City was appointed by a local associate architect, Jose Picciotto of Picciotto Arquitectos, who admires both Yeang's ecological approach and the intelligence and research that underscores it: 'Ken Yeang proposes a vertical urbanism, a theory which constitutes one of the best and most innovative solutions in these times. Growing cities upwards in order to stop "shaving" trees and using nature for the user's sake is something truly humane, which I personally share. What he has achieved is not for free. It constitutes years of work and research, plus a lot of logic due to his interest in offering a better comfort to the user; joining what nature dictates with a breakthrough design.'[16]

Picciotto's understanding of how best to engage Yeang's talents comes through in the final design for the tower. The scheme optimises Yeang's holistic ecological approach, creating a comfortable and attractive living environment for the residents. This is reflected in the interior and exterior planning of the block as well as its design. To give the apartments the best views (there are typically four units on each floor), they are placed at the corners of the building with the central core given over to circulation. Each flat is designed to be a crossover split-level, so that every unit has a view to the south. The apartments are naturally ventilated with evaporative cooling shafts. In addition to individual balconies there is a sky garden half the way up the tower that creates a recreational focus for the apartment community, and allows the residents to enjoy the verdant landscaping of this green tower.

Notes
1 Ken Yeang, 'Bases for Ecosystem Design', *AD*, July 1972. This was followed up two years later by Yeang with 'Energetics of the Built Environment', *AD*, July 1974.
2 Ken Yeang, 'A Theoretic Framework for the Incorporation of Ecological Considerations in the Design and Planning of the Built Environment', PhD dissertation, Cambridge University Library, England, 1981. (Published in the US in 1995 by McGraw-Hill as *Designing with Nature*.)
3 Leon van Schaik, 'The Biggest Party Wall in the World?', unpublished manuscript on Hamzah & Yeang's UMNO Tower in Penang, Malaysia.
4 Ibid.
5 Ivor Richards, *Groundscrapers and Subscrapers of Hamzah & Yeang*, Wiley-Academy, John Wiley & Sons (London), 2001.
6 For more on the development of Yeang's low-rise type, see ibid, pp 8–13.
7 Leon van Schaik, 'Simultaneity', *Ecocells*, John Wiley & Sons (London), 2003 (pages unnumbered).
8 For these insights I am indebted to Van Schaik and his unpublished manuscript 'The Biggest Party Wall in the World?'
9 Ibid.
10 Email from Christopher Chia to Helen Castle, 27 June 2003.
11 Van Schaik, 'Simultaneity', op cit.
12 Email from Yeang, 11 August 2003.
13 Ibid.
14 Here I paraphrase Yeang from my interview with him in London on 2 May 2003.
15 Quoting from my notes at the May 2003 interview with Yeang.
16 Email from Jose Picciotto to Helen Castle, 8 July 2003.
17 Quoting from my notes at the May 2003 interview with Yeang.
18 Email from Leon van Schaik to Helen Castle, 11 August 2003.
19 Email from Mohd Puzi Ahmad to Helen Castle, 11 July 2003.
20 Email from Ken Yeang to Helen Castle, 18 August 2003.
21 Email from Mohd Puzi Ahmad to Helen Castle, 11 July 2003.

Above right
The Menara Mesiniaga in Subang Jaya, completed in 1992. This was Yeang's second building for the company. The new building in Penang is his third.

Opposite
Rendering of the Penang building.

Inset
The new Mesiniaga building in Penang.

for the building. 'In principle, what the owner wants may not be what he needs. It is important to try and understand the crux of the problem and turn the creative process on its head.'[17]

To illustrate the importance of factoring the client–architect relationship in the architectural process, Yeang outlines three types of clients and examples of buildings that have been the upshot of each: 1) The client from the competition process. This is a lottery as client and architect are thrust upon each other. Unless a signature building is required, Yeang believes competitions are largely 'unjustified' as the client is better served by reviewing an architect's credentials and his or her track record; 2) The client who approaches Yeang precisely because he or she wants to acquire a green signature building; 3) Commercial clients who want to procure a marketable product at a predictable price.

To Conclude

To overemphasise the commercial aspects of Yeang's practice is in many ways to underestimate both the sophistication of his own ideas and the aspirations of his clients who in engaging Hamzah & Yeang are acknowledging that they require more than a strictly corporate architectural firm could deliver. As Leon van Schaik sums it up: 'The key to his [Yeang's] practice is that it is idea driven, and it provides benefits to clients through innovation rather than through an upfront demonstration of cheapness. His clients therefore tend to have more at stake than a quick return; they need to establish an image of themselves as progressive, ecologically responsible and of the future.'[18]

What Yeang has acquired by taking responsibility for costings from day one is a rare client confidence and understanding that has built up over three decades, as succinctly communicated by Puzi when he explains Mesiniaga's decision to give Yeang a repeat commission: 'Ken Yeang understands the business that we are in and our requirements.'[19] For as Yeang clearly concludes for me, the progress of a visionary architecture is in the built: 'We believe that no matter how exceptional is our design, if it does not meet the client's budget nor his requirements, then it will not get built. Why waste time and talent on unrealisable designs?'[20] △

For the content of this article, I am most grateful to Kenneth Yeang for giving up his time for an interview and for answering countless questions over email. I am also indebted to Leon van Schaik for his generosity in sending me his unpublished article, which has provided a springboard for many of the ideas contained here.

Commercial Client
The Mesiniaga Building, Penang
(completed March 2003)

Over the last 30 years, Hamzah & Yeang has designed three buildings for Menara Mesiniaga, the franchise owner of IBM (in addition to this newly completed building these are the 1985 IBM Plaza in Kuala Lumpur and the Menara Mesiniaga in Subang Jaya, completed in 1992). Mr Mohd Puzi Ahmad, the client of the building, clearly stated what his aims were when, on behalf of his company, he commissioned Yeang to design a new staff headquarters in Penang: 'The requirement for the Penang Project was to produce a building similar to the award-winning Menara Mesiniaga [in Subang Jaya], which will stand out as a landmark in Penang, but at a fraction of the cost. We wanted the Mesiniaga Penang building to reflect a sense of the corporate high-tech image in line with the business that Mesiniaga is in and in keeping with the image of the HQ facilities, in Subang Jaya.'[21]

In the Penang building, commercial interests and ecological considerations effectively converge. With its double-volume 'skycourts' on the first and second levels, and roof terrace and external louvres for solar-shading to reduce solar gain, the building embodies several of the principles of Yeang's bioclimatic approach for tall buildings. It also successfully fulfils the client's corporate requirements for its headquarters. As Puzi sums it up: 'The Penang facility has a practical and pleasing layout while still retaining the high-quality high-tech brand so closely associated with Mesiniaga Berhad.'

A Housing Boom
Embraces High Design

Above
Eisaku Ushida, Light Cave,
Tokyo, 2001. Developed by
Linea.

Opposite
Manabu Naya, Luceria House,
2001. Developed by Linea.

Tokyo is in the midst of a construction and development boom that threatens the city's quality of life. But a survey of the boom also uncovers a new, welcoming attitude towards good design. The economy's supply side has begun to recognise the market for excellent architecture, and although some property developers are executing 'design' in name only, other companies have made real contributions to the architectural landscape. The sea change is particularly notable in housing development, says **Masaaki Takahashi**, which has been a historical stronghold of conservative design.

Suppose you live in a classy low-rise house in a quiet residential area with abundant greenery in Tokyo. You enjoy a peaceful life there. But one day, high-rise condominiums, called 'mansions' in Japan, suddenly start mushrooming. These large-scale apartments more often than not ruin the landscape around you. They infringe on light and even cause TV interference. Some neighbourhood elementary schools do not have the capacity to house and teach the new pupils flooding in.

The Tokyo megalopolis has become such a forest of mansions. A recent explosion in development and construction has been described as the 'mini-bubble', after the bubble economy. The apartment market has been glutted for two years and it is certain that the supply of office buildings will exceed demand in 2003. The boom shows no sign of subsiding. And yet the mini-bubble comes at a time when huge debts from the bubble economy have yet to be settled. Moreover, Japan's is an ageing society with a declining birth rate.

At the heart of the mini-bubble is collusion between politics and business. The Koizumi cabinet's Urban Redevelopment Law, for example, is the finishing touch to the government's 30-year-long land-use policy of virtually unrestricted deregulation. It allows practically anything to be built in Tokyo. To promote urban housing, high-rise residence promotion districts with an allowable floor area ratio of 600 per cent are designated in areas where the ratio was previously 400 per cent – and corridors and stairs are excluded in the calculation.

Moreover, government- and media-generated publicity claiming that now is the best time to buy houses is dangerous. Journalists report on properties without mentioning the overall risks of the mini-bubble. Housing-information magazines are flooded with fashionable landscapes and lifestyles. But the stance is clearly shortsighted and threatens future citizens and leaders of Tokyo with cleaning up after the economic and quality-of-life problems that are left behind.

Changing Attitudes Towards Architecture
Japanese developers fall into two categories: those affiliated with construction companies and others with real-estate companies. The former are making great efforts to reduce construction costs in the present recession. The latter are more sales-oriented and put greater emphasis on design; however, more often than not, though these companies advertise the names of architects invited to their projects, we rarely hear those names beyond a project's planning stage. This is because the demands of developers and estate agents prevent the architects from doing what they want to. And without the true involvement of architects, the final product tends to be banal.

Major developers' mansions have been selling conservative designs and luxury, with middle- and small-scale condominiums following the same architectural grammar.

The trend dates back to 1955 when the Japan Housing Corporation, now called the Urban Development Corporation, was established. The organisation popularised modern housing complexes; private-sector collective housing wasn't developed until after the 1970s. However, the entire supply side's attitude towards design remains as rigid as it was before the Second World War. Floor plans and interiors reflected economic efficiency, not dwellers' desires, for example. The layout was schematically represented by a combination of the number of rooms and three letters, L, D and K – living room, dining room and kitchen, respectively. So 2DK, for instance, means two bedrooms and a dining room cum kitchen.

The Japan Housing Corporation proposed a separation of the dining room and bedroom as the model for a new lifestyle. However, the xLDK layout was not well suited to the Japanese lifestyle. The traditional Japanese room is flexible by nature, and can be used according to the time of day and the occasion. The notation restricts the form of housing and apartments are sometimes divided into tiny rooms. But more rooms do not necessarily equate to more space – in fact, a seemingly large 2LDK (two bedrooms, living room and dining room/kitchen) apartment is usually too small

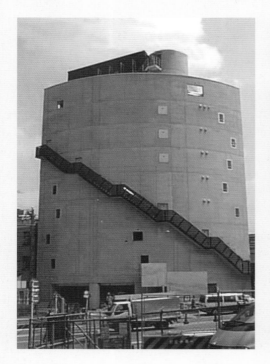

for the purported separation of rooms to improve users' quality of life.

The supply side also tended to give only secondary consideration to the aspects that were not captured by the xLDK notation. Developers tried to construct as many housing units as possible on a site, which not only resulted in these small carved-up apartments, but also in poor communal space and amenities.

Despite the complaints against the typology raised by longtime and prospective residents alike, developers rigidly adhered to the almost formalist xLDK notation in the name of streamlined development and economies of scale. Furthermore, more elaborate designs meant high maintenance costs, while purchasers tended to prefer conservatism. Such considerations have made the design of housing complexes unattractive and restrictive to the majority of architects, and instead these projects have poured into the hands of businesses which specialise in them, and the design departments of general contractors. Here, architects work subordinately to the clients, creating a vicious circle that further compromises the design. (This is less often the case with rental apartments.)

However, developers know they are at a turning point – and the mini-bubble reflects this. Mori

Building Co Ltd is a leading developer and proprietary company in charge of dry-as-dust office buildings in Tokyo. But after designing and completing Ark Hills, a 'city within a city' consisting of a skyscraper, concert hall, luxury apartment building and commercial complex, the firm started to become more and more design oriented.

As part of an image-branding campaign, Mori's Tokyo projects have championed architecture in the last few years. The company appointed Cesar Pelli to design Atago Green Hills, completed in 2001. And Moto-azabu Hills, completed the following year, boasts Terence Conran-designed decor.

Most recently, Mori's Roppongi Hills received enormous media attention on its completion in April 2003. It is one of the largest building complexes, with a total area of approximately 11.6 hectares and a floor area of about 724,000 square metres, and is twice as large as Ark Hills. Roppongi contains 54-storey office buildings, a TV station, hotel and museum of art. To create a one-of-a-kind attractive block, Mori's design department employed many brand designers from overseas, including Kohn Pederson Fox

Above and right
Mnabu Chiba, Split, Tokyo, 2002.
Developed by Takagi Planning Office.

Opposite
Akio Yachida/Workshop, Torre Vista, Tokyo, 2003. Developed by Takagi Planning Office.

Associates, Jerde Partnership International, Inc, Maki and Associates, Gluckman Mayner Architects and Conran & Partners. Although the company says the project is viable, the office building was actually over budget, which indicates that higher priority was given to differentiating it in a saturated market.

Meanwhile, the Shimizu Corporation, a major construction company, chose the Aldo Rossi Office as design supervisor of the Crest Tower, a 32-storey building it has developed and now manages. Rossi has passed away but his brand is immortal! Real-estate giant Sumitomo Real Estate Sales Co Ltd didn't hesitate to invite maestro Tadao Ando to design his first housing complex in Tokyo, in order not to miss out on the trend. This marked the beginning of the consumption of architect brands in collective housing, which was until so recently beleaguered by efficiency engineering.

Furthermore, estate agents are beginning to meet the design-conscious demand that contributes to a higher standard of collective housing. The trend is also spurred by the increasing popularity of co-operative houses, built by groups of prospective residents. And architect-initiated renovations of older buildings are also catching the interest of consumers.

This design consciousness is now especially evident in magazines which target the general reader, rather than in housing magazines. Among these are *Brutus* and its sister magazine *Casa Brutus*. Since the 1980s, *Brutus* has been attempting to make it hip for young businesspeople to talk about architecture and to make architects more visible to the public. Along with other similar magazines, it exposes the architects more than their works, almost to the point of excess, transforming Le Corbusier and Ando into brand symbols like Gucci and Prada.

While perhaps occasionally superficial, these publications should at least be credited with making the work of architects more open to general interest. For example, the 1 November 2002 issue of *Brutus* featured a bold project in which Ando, Jean Nouvel and Steven Holl would create housing complexes for readers. A similar project was realised for detached houses. Other issues cover architecture from different angles, such as introducing promising architects by presenting virtual projects.

Against this background the phrase 'designer mansion' has recently been coined. It refers to the fashionable apartment houses that trend-conscious younger generations want to live in. But, just as magazines have sometimes reduced architecture to a fashion label, 'designer' buildings often aren't designed at all, and their bare concrete walls are disappointing. In the 1980s, 'designer brand' was a buzzword for youngsters, who squandered their money on clothes. And since the 1990s we have been

in a 'designer restaurant' boom. In the midst of the designer mansion fad, it is uncertain how strong the general consciousness will be towards dwellings. Still, it is important to note that since the late 1990s some of the rich young customers, educated by *Brutus* and eschewing mere trends, would like, and can afford, to live in design-conscious residences.

Appropriately, then, although the fad has bolstered those developers who peddle high design only nominally, Japan is also home to some truly progressive collective housing. To find it you have to search among the works of a small number of medium- and small-sized developers and architectural consulting businesses. (Projects by government corporations and local governments that involve up-and-coming architects like Kazuyo Sejima are also on the increase.) For example, Fukuoka Jisho Co Ltd, a developer/estate agent based in Fukuoka, Kyushu, is taking part in giant commercial complexes like the Canal City project in Fukuoka, as well as waterfront projects and housing developments.

For Fukuoka Jisho's Nexus World project, completed in 1991, Steven Holl, Rem Koolhaas,

Above and right
Akio Yachida/Workshop, Loops, Tokyo, 1999. Developed by Takagi Planning Office.

Opposite
Yuuji Sekine, Crevice, Tokyo, 2001. Developed by Takagi Planning Office.

Mark Mack, Osamu Ishiyama, Christian de Portzamparc and Oscar Tusquets, under Arata Isozaki as co-ordinator, were each was asked to design one building. Their works line up in a row over 5 hectares within the total site area of 9,947 square metres. The building area is 2,033 square metres and the total floor area 14,330 square metres with 250 dwelling units. The neighbourhood is punctuated by the Nexus Momomichi Residential Tower, which was designed by Michael Graves. Each building has its own style so there is no sense of overall harmony, making the project look like a housing exhibition.

The Takagi Planning Office in Harajuku, one of Tokyo's most fashionable neighbourhoods, is another such real-estate agent. Its CEO, Eiichi Takagi, who established the company in 1997, is often featured in *Brutus* and other magazines. The company is renowned for the design-conscious apartments, both for rent and ownership, that it commissions architects to design. Its portfolio of architects has yet to include any big names, but all are reputed to be talented and promising. Takagi says that so far rental housing has been unattractive, and that 1990s apartment houses

by developers, as well as eccentric architect-designed housing complexes, have stressed conspicuousness over comfort. He believes that appealing design and harmony with the streetscape will become part of the asset value of buildings, and he dares to ignore market research which tends to kill creativity and new products. 'It's important to educate the market by showing it advanced models and good results,' he says. 'Planners and co-ordinators have not been given the position they deserve so far. Recent appreciation of our works clearly indicates an increasing need for them.'

In a chic black building in a residential district about 20 minutes' walk from the Takagi Planning Office is estate agent/co-ordinator Linea Co Ltd. Established in 1988, Linea deals in sophisticated properties and is often featured in the international media. Like Takagi's office it commissions projects to excellent architects. 'Designer apartment houses are getting a lot of media attention and are now widely known,' says CEO Miyuki Sakano, 'but when we started our business in the late 1980s they were known only to a small number of insiders and didn't even have a name.' The increasing availability of information on housing in the media, as well as more diverse lifestyles, has meant that

Nexus Housing Complex competition, Fukuoka City, 1991, developed by Fukuoka Jisho Co Ltd, co-ordinated by Arata Isozaki

Above right
Housing designed by Christian de Portzamparc.

Right
Housing designed by Mark Mack.

Far right
Housing designed by Oscar Tusquets.

design-conscious consumer demand is now overwhelming developers' supply.

Sakano goes on to point out that the popularity of designer rental apartments and co-operative houses shares the same roots. Dwellers are becoming more and more dissatisfied with 'ready-made-ness' and superficiality and more and more aware of their own styles as yardsticks. 'I feel consumers are interested not only in low prices and freedom of design but also in the sense of urban community. The future of designer apartments completely depends on how we understand and express this concept,' he says.

While these projects are feeding the demand for identity through design, what they are only beginning to contemplate is how to resolve the ramifications of the mini-bubble. Takagi is negative about the government's wholesale deregulation and has doubts about high-rise buildings. He believes that housing complexes should be low enough for the residents to feel nature. 'Recently the media often emphasises a view, especially a night view, as a requirement for collective housing,' he says, 'but it's more important how you incorporate nature into your apartments and how you harmonise them with the neighbourhood.' Sakano also points out the danger of unsophisticated 'mansions' destroying the neighbourhood, and sees the restoration of a sense of community in co-operative housing projects as a real possibility for the future. ⌂

Above left
Nexus housing designed by
Osamu Ishiyama.

Above right
Nexus housing designed by
Rem Koolhaas.

Bottom left
Nexus housing designed by
Steven Holl.

Melbourne

(Lc

Napier Street Housing, designed by Kerstin Thompson Architects, represents a trend in Melbourne's inner-city densification. **Leon van Schaik** explains how, because it stands out, it cuts across a trend towards architectural excellence, pre-empting new design standards that consumers are just beginning to demand.

Australian cities grow according to a disarmingly simple urban pattern. Annular rings of growth ripple out from the founding settlement on a steady trajectory that is followed by a second wave of denser subdivisions over the original core. The value curves are high in the middle and cascade down to the perimeter in a trade-off between cheap land and expensive transport. Redundant facilities in the centre become residential complexes.

Melbourne's population of 3.5 million is sprawling, following the desirable Mornington Peninsula south and east of the central business district. Since 1997, when planning controls were devolved to local councils, the city has grown by around 300 square kilometres a year and now covers 7,700 square kilometres. An Australian discussion of housing is very properly couched in terms of the quarter-acre block, therefore, and its continuance largely invokes dreams of individual paradises that date to the aspirations of the Chartist movement of the 1830s.

Rising

W)

Australians are not ignorant of the pleasures of the city. Indeed, they manufacture cities with Breughelesque densities when they holiday, as many do, in vast caravan camps in the mountains and at coastal resorts. And the inner city attracts thousands of weekend visitors from the thinly populated margins who come to experience the cosmopolitan jostling and socialisation that commuting robs them of.

Periodically, too, there are waves of densification. Seamus O'Hanlan has shown that in 1947, 20 per cent and 13.5 per cent of the populations of Sydney and Melbourne, respectively, lived in inner-suburban apartments or their precursors – boarding houses. In the late 1960s, half of all house starts in Sydney and Melbourne were in 'six pack' units, with two storeys of apartments over parking.[1]

In the 1980s property slump that followed a wave of office construction in downtown Melbourne, the city introduced its Postcode 3000 project. These measures softened some development controls in order to stimulate conversion of the previous boom's empty office buildings into apartments. This flowed into a new boom that has yet to peak. In 1999, the City of Melbourne could assert that 18.6 per cent of the core and inner-suburb populations lived in medium- to higher-density housing. Furthermore, 20,000 units were completed in Melbourne last year, and a similar number is in the pipeline for each of the next four years.

In this current boom, some of the best urban-core projects are architect developed, a process initiated in this generation by Nonda Katsalidis, whose Melbourne Terrace development began a trend towards well-designed new apartments in the city centre. Although architects design only 8 per cent of all Australian housing, architect-led development is something of a tradition in Melbourne, as O'Hanlan shows: architect Howard Lawson caught the Hollywood mood between

GROUND FLOOR

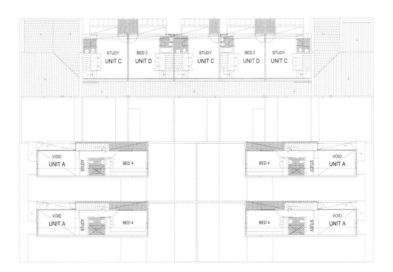

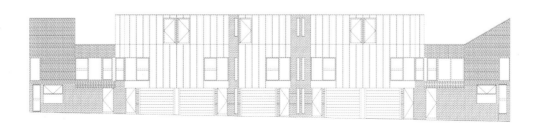

1922 and 1941, building 200 flats in a Beverly Hills mansion style. And Best Overend built an innovative, minimally planned courtyard complex called 'Cairo' on the edge of Fitzroy in 1933, which shows a clear influence by European planning.

There are several types of consumer drawn to such inner-city housing. They include married couples whose children have left home and who are opting for a central-city lifestyle, young urban professionals and investors, most typically from Singapore. The developments in which these demographics are now purchasing units are European-inspired architecturally, but not all boast architectural excellence. Rather, most buildings are styled rather than designed. Specifically, the apparent utility of spaces is more symbolic than real, with unsuitable balconies, tight and conventionally planned spaces, inconvenient split levels and the pointy 'features' that Robyn Boyd critiqued in the 1950s and 1960s.

Napier Street

Napier Street Housing, designed by Kerstin Thompson Architects (KTA), is located in Fitzroy, Melbourne's first suburb. Considering this placement, it ranks as one of the many projects produced by the current inner-city housing boom.

It is important to note that Fitzroy was the last neighbourhood to embody an 18th-century urban model of mixed development. Grand terrace houses for the wealthy line its major streets, rising to five storeys at corners. Mews and workers' cottages occupy the areas behind, and a comprehensive mixture of shops, workshops and factories spreads throughout, with shops clustered along tram routes. This mix has made Fitzroy a vital part of the city's cultural life, as

architects, designers and artists have found different rental and spatial niches for their activities at different stages in their careers.

A large tract between Brunswick Street (the north–south tram route) and Napier Street (a quiet, tree-lined residential street of middle-income houses), however, was demolished and replaced with 20-storey Housing Commission blocks. This is Napier Street Housing's neighbour to the west.

The site is on the corner with Webb Street, in which Thompson did an early renovation that opened up an internalised house to sky and yard without disrupting the streetscape, and at the far end of which the architect has her office in an old bank chamber. There are handsome brick warehouses and factories on the other flanks, and the characteristic patchwork of the 'sanitary' night soil laneways has become a network of pedestrian and cycle routes lined with corrugated iron fences, blank brick walls and a huge variety of trees and climbing plants.

Resolving Complexity with Distinction

Shane Murray has observed that with Napier Street Housing Thompson 'develops aims that she has often articulated: the idea of the "interstitial" as a mode of thinking around architecture, and a preference for hybrid and complex solutions rather than singular utterances.' The architect argues that the project 'is a cost-effective development which consists of 11 dwellings with seemingly spacious proportions, generous roof terraces and flexible options for occupation.'

Opposite, top
Ground-floor, first-floor and mezzanine plans of houses.

Opposite, bottom
Napier Street and Webb Street elevations.

Above left
Aerial view of town houses.

Above right
View of houses down Webb Street.

Designed for a local estate-agent client who rents out apartments not used by family members, the project is a family affair. One of the client's cousins built it, and the client handled contract administration. In this spirit, Thompson's practice was, she believes, selected because it is located on the same street as the site.

Thompson reports her surprise at the ease with which the project received its planning and building permits. This is probably because the building has such strong continuities with its context. Indeed, Thompson says she drew upon the 'formal, material and typological traits of Fitzroy' to create 'an intervention that is irreducibly local and specific' based on the '19th-century terrace slivers'. She says that the project is 'in dialogue rather than denial' in that 'the housing produces a resonance with its surroundings by insinuating difference rather than simplistic contextual deference'.

Thompson loves the way the afternoon sunlight amplifies the redness of the bricks in Fitzroy. She recounts how her family had designed brick kilns in Central Europe, and how, on a visit, she tracked down the old brickworks. The site was overgrown with trees and a few bricks lay amongst their roots. She laughs, recalling the experience of explaining the bricks to customs officials.

Echoing these European bricks, the facade of Napier Street Housing includes pavers to achieve an alternative scaling of the red bookends; black bricks form the base of the building. The combination of zinc roof sheeting, acrylic screens and brick allows people to identify their own apartments. They have warehouse-type interiors and warehouse-profile sections 'that give you light and a robust exterior; the inside is up to you.'

These apparently heterogeneous materials also fit unobtrusively, even sympathetically, within the surroundings. At first glance it is difficult to see that there is something new here. The architect cites Alison and Peter Smithson: 'The project is also an act of urbanism – a demonstration of how a building today is interesting only if it is more than itself; if it charges the space around it with connective possibilities.' She is determined that the architecture resonates with the lanes and the Housing Commission blocks, and scales to them in the overall form of the profile of the building. The profile breaks up into readily recognisable unit-size components, but has a vigour that avoids the risk of looking effete beside the Brutalist hulk of the tall buildings.

There are three types of dwelling: the largest (four in number, occupied by the owners) run east–west across the rear of the site, and there is a corner type (two in

number) and a north–south type facing Webb Street between the corners (the remaining five units). Bulk is concentrated along the edges of the site and is reduced to the centre to allow good sun penetration to private, upper-level outdoor terraces.

Energy performance is addressed through orientation, with sunlight penetration to the upper floors, concrete floors as heat sinks, cross-flow ventilation, appropriate insulation in walls and floors and materials selected for long life and low maintenance. In a recent report the architects state: 'The relationship between practice and developer is very good post-completion. The occupants' feedback is that the units are very livable and can easily accommodate a variety of household types. The community reaction that we have received first-hand is generally very positive and there is a genuine appreciation for the quality of the project, particularly in consideration to the impact it has on three streets ... The breakdown of the building bulk to Little George Street (the laneway) allowed for three-storey development without undermining the amenity of private open space to the rear of the George Street properties.'

And so KTA's Napier Street Housing is an atypical work. Although it is located in the city core like so much other new housing in Melbourne, its intelligent design is remarkably different from the styling that trumps so many other contemporary developments. The Napier Street Housing has a sureness of touch that only such works as 'Altair' by Engelen Moore in Sydney match in its economy and authority. Not coincidentally, both architects come to housing from designing individual houses, the robust usability and internal amenities of which are clearly apparent in Napier Street.

Kerstin Thompson Architect's next inner-city project is Interval at QV, a crèche, car park and office building. This building, Thompson says, is not so much a design of spaces between buildings as an interval building. Her aim here echoes what has been achieved at Napier Street Housing:

'Our interest is in orchestrating a multidimensional experience of architecture – one that is effective and connective beyond the immediate site. Sometimes this demands quietness and positioning of the building as an interval – the point that negotiates between differences and that figures architecture as the means to highlighting the evolving and shifting conditions of the built fabric of our cities and constructed environments. The notion of building as interval is critical to understanding architecture as one moment of many that, in sequence, orchestrate a larger topographic landscape, for example. It is a counter-argument to the reduction of architecture to icon in the fashioning of our cities.' ⌐⌐

Opposite, bottom left
View from Napier Street.

Opposite, bottom right
View from Webb Street.

Above
Napier Street view.

Note
1 Seamus O'Hanlan, *Together Apart: Boarding House, Hostel and Flat Life in Pre-War Melbourne*, Australian Scholarly Publishing (Melbourne), 2002.

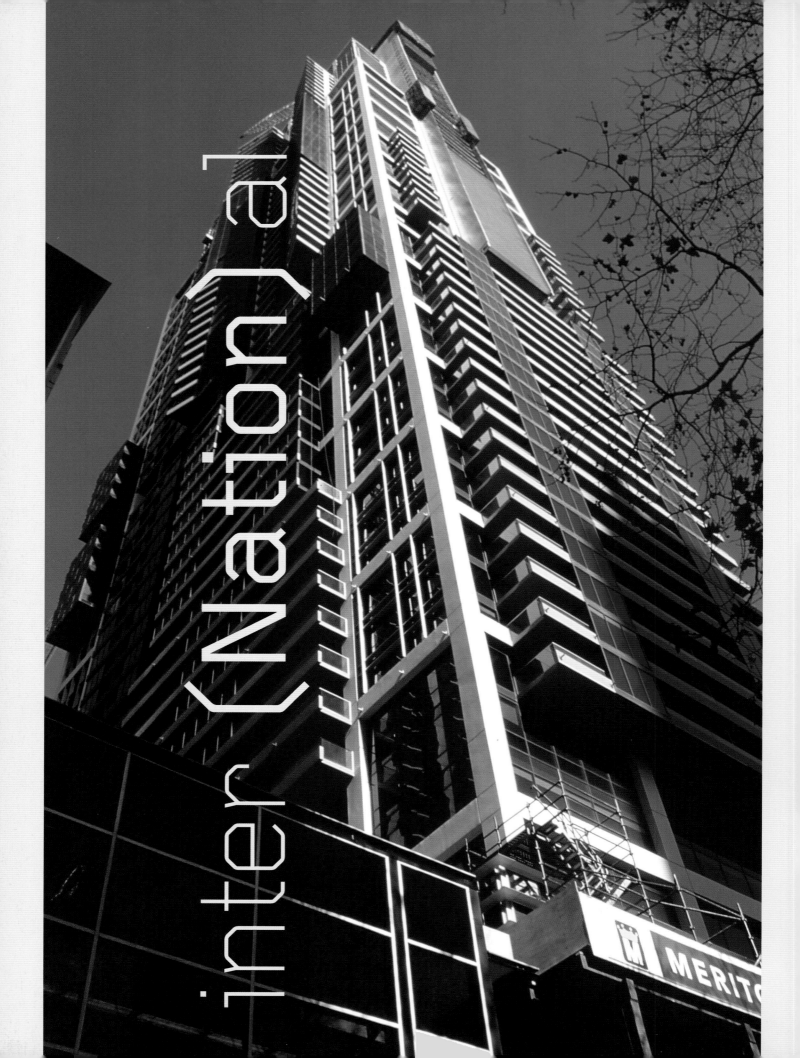

The education and career of Bob Nation can be easily deemed peripatetic but, as **Stephen Varady** explains, this architect's nomadic lifestyle has paid off. By developing a portfolio of work in regions more accepting of complex super-sized construction, Nation was well placed to become the designer of choice for large-scale developers, both Australian and international, on his return home.

For Modernist architect Bob Nation, a formative period's frustration with Australia – its scale and challenges, or lack thereof – gave birth to a career. His architectural studies began in Tasmania, Australia, in 1961, but quickly bored by the experience he travelled to Toronto on scholarship. Inspired teaching by the likes of George Baird, Peter Pragnell and John Andrews provided him with a healthy dose of idealism and on returning to Tasmania he started the practice of Heffernan, Nation, Rees in 1973, which later became Heffernan, Nation, Viney (the practice of teaming with one or two partners another recurring theme). In Tasmania, Nation pursued his Modernist direction through smaller-scale residential and commercial projects, and unhappy with the small-town mentality moved to Hong Kong in 1980.

Hong Kong may have created some culture shock, but it also introduced Nation to the challenges he sought. Working on larger projects with Yuncken Freeman (which became PDCM) and Liang Peddle Thorp, Nation recalls Hong Kong in the early 1980s: 'Hong Kong was an immersion into the commerciality of that environment, where buildings were transitory and the substance of any development was about the cost of the land and the constraints placed on it by government. One learned to try and be creative within incredibly strict controls regarding form and content.' Speaking of 'commercially creative' clients as well as 'one of the most difficult and complex underground substrata circumstances in the world,' Nation says of the experience: 'It also taught me to work at a very large scale; to go from houses in Hobart to new towns in Hong Kong was quite a step.'

The period took Nation from Tokyo to London and back to Hong Kong, when one of his contacts approached him about designing a new town in Bangkok. Understandably, 'It was an unbelievable opportunity that just came out of the blue. As an individual given the responsibility to master-plan a new town it was just a unique experience that allowed me to realise the kinds of things we'd talked about previously in Malaysia and China but never realised, but again, within an incredibly tight commercial circumstance.'

With new partner Karl Fender, Nation built a 100-person team. 'One of the major events that influenced

Opening page
World Tower, Sydney, July
2003. East and north
elevations under construction.

Previous page
Bob Nation (right) and Karl
Fender (left) in their Bangkok
office in 1991.

Above left
Flatted factories, Muang Thong
Thani, Bangkok, 1990–3. Eight
buildings of 50,000 square
metres per building house six
factory levels with recreation
facilities (including tennis
courts) on the roof decks.

Above right
Nation House, Sandy Bay,
Tasmania, 1976–8.

the process and the product,' he says, 'was that I brought the construction companies – Bouygues from France and Leightons from Australia – into the equation. Each had a different point of view but still all of the buildings we realised were very much born out of construction attitudes and delivery processes that we developed with them. We realised impossible programmes and developed a sophistication of construction techniques and methods that didn't exist in Thailand before then.' Indeed, in addition to high-standard industrial units, the project's residential towers also created a precedent for Thailand.

Returning to Australia five years ago, where the partnership became Nation Fender Katsalidis, based in Melbourne, he worked on numerous large residential projects (some of which are only now coming to light) as well as the Sidney Myer Asia Centre for Melbourne University.

Just over three years ago he won a design competition for the tallest residential tower in Sydney and the southern hemisphere. The client, Meriton, had a reputation for low-scale and low-budget housing developments. Meriton had bought a very large site in the centre of the city that had sat empty for over 15 years since the boom period of the 1980s. Thus the new project, now known as World Tower, was a shift in scale and design aesthetic for the company.

The initial impetus for creating an architect-designed building came from Sydney City Council. The lord mayor, Frank Sartor, with incredible influence from councillor (and practising architect) Graham Jahn, had recently instigated a design-competition process within the city in a very serious attempt to improve Sydney's built environment. The World Tower site happened to be the first to fall under the auspices of the council's new policy – a policy which also stipulates that the design architect must continue through the construction phase of the project to ensure design integrity.

Nation explains his design strategy: 'Fundamentally, the design for World Tower was about de-imaging the building, to place it apart from the "normal" Sydney buildings which, regardless of their materiality, were just simple extrusions from ground to top. So the fundamental philosophy was about trying to establish three different scalings which related to the three different scales of the city – the 25- to 30-storey stuff, the 55- to 60-storey stuff and then that which was above as a different reading altogether. This was the way, I thought, to give it a point of difference within the physical and formal image of the city.

'I also wanted to break down the single-storey scale of this type of residential building,' he continues, 'by giving it a broader urban scale; this was done with the superframe at three storeys. Then its visual complexity was increased through the various

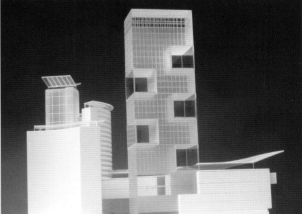

Above
Skytrain, Bangkok, 1996.
Model of winning competition
submission for a new
town for 300,000 people over
a new train depot.

Far right, top
Cathay Cinema site
redevelopment, Kuala Lumpur,
1996. Model of winning
competition submission.

Right
Model of Stelux office building,
Hong Kong, 1995–8.

Far right, bottom
Nation apartment/warehouse
conversion, Fitzroy, Melbourne,
Australia, 1991–3. View of living
area, courtyard and bathroom.
Royal Australian Institute of
Architects Award winner 1993.

balcony and winter-garden elements that had their own "zipper-type" references on the facade. Finally, the three parts – bottom, middle and top – were connected by the continuous winter-garden elements on the east and west sides.'

The project is due for completion at the end of 2004, and has been a battle of wills between architect and client. Despite this, World Tower will be one of the most handsome on the Sydney skyline and is testament to Nation's experience in creating complex, articulated, well-planned buildings for financially driven clients.

Now living in Sydney, Nation has been working on projects ranging from single residences to massive urban design projects in China and Dubai. 'I find in Sydney that there is the beginning of a new opportunity of working from Sydney to the Middle East,' he says. Every design directly in his charge reflects his distinctly modern sensibilities and his clever, instinctive and successful planning methodologies and design approach.

So how does he make inroads with clients? Now well versed in the ways of development in all parts of the world, and with a totally charming demeanour, he creates a comfortable atmosphere for initial client dialogue. His knowledge about precedent and typologies is broad, and those years of (multinational

Right
Villa offices, Muang Thong Thani, Bangkok, 1990–4. The project consists of 92 contemporary reinterpretations of the traditional Thai shophouse. The six-, seven- and eight-storey buildings include a continuous basement car-park level, ground-floor retail level and three, four or five storeys of offices, all with two-storey apartments on top.

Below
Bird's-eye view of initial master plan for a new town for 500,000 people, Muang Thong Thani, Bangkok, 1990.

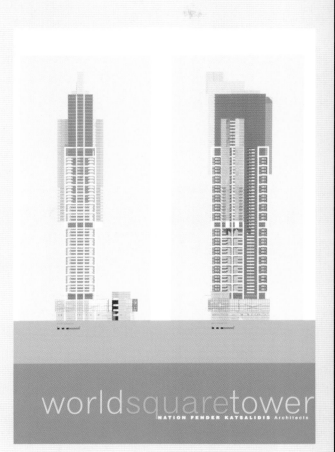

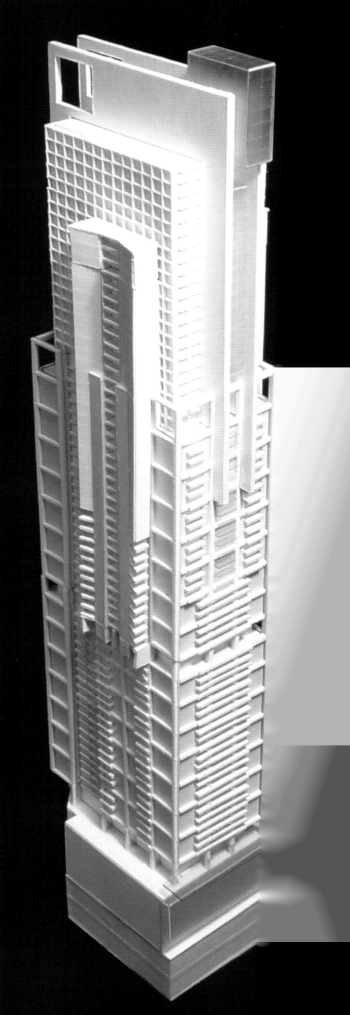

World Tower, Sydney, 2000

Above
Competition drawings of the
86-storey, 700-apartment
residential tower.

Right
West and south elevations
under construction.

Far right
Model of winning competition
submission.

and multicultural) practice have honed his schematic design skills to a rapidly accurate level, allowing him to successfully design and revise ideas on the run or on the fly, depending on where and how he happens to be travelling at the time. These skills give him an extremely strong base to work from so that even when the going gets tough with developer, builder or authorities, he generally manages to carve a positive path.

With such broad experience it is surprising to hear his pointed observations about working in Sydney: 'The major thing about Sydney that is different from any other place is the intrusion of the politics. Specifically in terms of the review and approval process, which is entirely different to anything I've ever worked with. It is far more interfering and conditioning than anything in Australia and also anything overseas that I've ever experienced.'

In architecture circles, Nation is still young at 60 years of age, and he finds himself in a position of respect within the Australian architectural profession. Yet he is not solely concerned about his own welfare and believes in patronage and mentoring within the profession of architecture: 'So much of the incredibly talented architectural youth of Sydney – and I mean everyone from 30 to 50 – has never had the opportunity to develop into larger-scale projects. My desire is to try to find a route to develop that talent and somehow downgrade the impact of the large practices that have moderated the quality of the city.' ⌂

Victoria Park project, Sydney, 2002–04+

Above
Block designed with Peter Wilson.

Right, top
West elevation of tower block overlooking the central park.

Right, bottom
Detail study of apartments.

Homes for China

In what observers may deem a Chinese Postmodernism, property developers have responded to the new capitalism by unleashing a torrent of eclecticism in the architecture of private housing. As **Laurent Gutierrez** and **Valérie Portefaix** of Hong-Kong based Map Office explain, this new paradigm is best represented by Hong Kong's high-density towers which, despite innumerable stylistic references to history and fantasy, actually render the architect moot.

Previous page
New town, Tsuen Kwan 0, private block entrance.

Above
Hong Kong is reputed to have one of the highest population densities in the world. The vertical compression of the population is balanced by a large number of services and equipments, both public and private. Hong Kong vertical footprint studies the amount of available space per person in Hong Kong and the different types of services necessary to each urban scale. This analysis aims to identify a series of urban standards (public housing estate, 9 square metres per person; private housing estate, 4 square metres per person) and is inspired by the research of Paul Nelson, 'Towards the Creation of Urban Standard' (1943), which was published in *L'Architecture d'Aujourd'hui*, July 1947.

China's transition to a capitalist economy has only exacerbated the hyperdensity of Hong Kong. And the local property development industry is catering to the desires of newly wealthy citizens to escape from this urban environment. Surveying the general architectural principles that underlie new private residential developments shows that architects – as visionaries for solving future land-use problems or expressing individual identity – are being superseded by seemingly Postmodern manifestations of collective fantasy.

Massive residential tower blocks have infiltrated Hong Kong's territory like a forest, heedless of geography. A view from the mountain peaks reveals a violent contrast between the dense high-rise developments and the natural island/mountain setting. From this evident juxtaposition, there is no doubt that lack of land and a growing population have provided the perfect context with which to experiment with new forms of densities.

Land use and verticality are not the only vectors that set up Hong Kong's urban condition. Optimisation drives the region to expand activities and movements at any level of infrastructure, voids or building blocks. The most dynamic form of such density has found a new extreme in Great Harbor View, the most recent 72-storey private residential model.

Hong Kong's public housing policy is in part responsible for its fundamental system of density, connectivity, intensity, speculation and new living conditions. Hong Kong initiated its public housing programme after the disastrous Shek Kip Mei fire killed hundreds of squatters following the end of the Pacific War. It now shelters almost 3.5 million people, or approximately half of the territorial population. Starting with a goal of 'temporary safe housing of a minimum standard', initial efforts focused on providing collective basic services and modest private living space. Even in the first permanent blocks and estates, tenants had to share water, and toilets and cooking facilities were found in communal balconies.

Ground-floor shops and rooftop kindergartens usually completed the elementary planning and indeed, from the original 'Mark 1' housing schemes to the latest cruciform-tower 'harmony blocks', the solid organisation of collective services has always countered a clear lack of individual space and privacy.

The standard to achieve high-density developments starts with the residential unit. The number of people living in a unit is constant throughout the territory, but the size of the unit varies considerably, from 300 to 2,000 square feet. This variation depends on the promoters' choice and results from market demands. In Hong Kong, half of the total population lives in public housing. Calculation of the number of people living in a unit takes into account domestic servants, the elderly and other family members.

Population 5   Area 600 square feet   1 residential unit

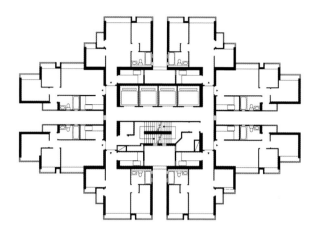

The organisation of a plan is based on the interlocking of eight apartments around a central core. To achieve a higher design efficiency, units are often mirrored two by two so that each floor plan proposes four different types of organisation. The effectiveness of the floor plan curtails circulation space in the unit and in the core. This constraint produces little privacy within the flat and between adjacent flats.

Population 40   Area 5,000 square feet   8 residential units

The Hong Kong residential tower block is the most standard building throughout the territory. Its verticality – now up to 72 storeys in Tim Sha Tsui – is enhanced by the repetition of the irregular silhouettes of identical floors. The replication of standard openings (windows or bay windows) usually ignores both orientation and context. The visible air-conditioning units and external piping add another layer of complexity to the facade. To carry out the vertical stacking of the floor plans, a horizontal link with the exterior or other towers is located at the lobby level.

Population 2,000
Area 5,000 square feet
(x 54 storeys)
432 residential units

The estate forms a large complex surrounded by tall walls that give the impression of an autonomous urban enclave. In a way it is a contemporary version of the traditional Chinese walled village. This implies a clear hierarchical spatial order from public to private that includes a number of social interactions and services. These transitions take place in the podium, which replaces the commercial-use ground floor.

Population 16,000
Area 2 hectares
3,456 residential units

Located in the northwestern New Territories, Tin Shui Wai, developed in the early 1990s, is Hong Kong's eighth new town. Built on land reclaimed from fish ponds, its 220 hectares now house about 187,000 people. The residents live in a mixture of public and private residential estates. By the end of 2003, Tin Shui Wai will be linked to the KCRC West Rail and its population is expected to increase to about 300,000 by 2009.

Population 160,000
Area 200 hectares
27,648 residential units

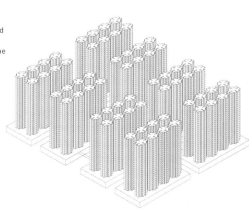

To conduct such large-scale plans, the public sector has developed prefabricated factory-made components for construction. And so, despite its problems, standardised models have rapidly colonised each connected part of the territory.

Recently, the private sector has adopted similar typologies, but with a range of programmes that go far beyond public housing's basic prototype. Derived from the newly capitalist, competitive economy, the planning of private residential developments directly reflects the erratic demands of the real-estate market. It does so, specifically, with cleverly packaged marketing concepts, each of which claims that the product has invented a new utopia for living.

In the arena of private housing speculation, architecture is no longer the art of designing buildings. Rather, it provides the means to support these expressions of exclusivity and collective fantasy. Each residential development forms a group of towers mounted on a podium where a highly diverse range of activities takes place. The physical structure of these complexes is repetitive, autonomous and hermetic. The residential dwelling units are more or less the same and the podium becomes the major selling point and experimental field. It is presented as a colossal house but with the preserved atmosphere of a private villa.

Like theme parks, the banal podium is embellished by walls, lights, mirrors, water and sounds-decorative elements that refer to both fashionable style and to images of luxury. This reminds and reinforces residents of their status, and prevalent clichés dominate. Developers lure buyers with images that borrow from Hawaiian resorts, utopian gardens, medieval castles and ancient Greece, as well as the Spanish, Renaissance and Baroque styles. The marketing vocabulary further flatters the potential client. In its brochure the Castello promotes a 'Royal sentiment, an Imperial attention, an Aristocratic enjoyment, the Envy of Royalty, a Noble style, a Royal residence providing luxurious living fit for a King.' To some extent this superficial interpretation of a theme and endless combination of styles has originated an aesthetic in response to capitalist China's new delocalised condition.

Private residential developments are usually built on prized sites: isolated yet well-connected locations that recall propaganda images of the solitary block erected in the middle of a rural jungle. Wherever it is located in the territory, each development competes for both the best natural scenery and the fastest connection: 'Situated on the coast of Castle Peak Road, the views from the property can be described as heavenly, and not to be found anywhere else. Mountains and oceans gently wrap themselves around the entire property. Gaze towards the north and see the beautiful Tam Lam Chung Reservoir and Tai Lam Country Park. And if you

Tsuen Kwan O under construction.

enjoy plane or car spotting, the airport and the North Lantau Expressway is right in front of your eyes.'

In the spirit of isolation, the height of the perimeter wall and the security gates that follow it appear to be directly inspired by the medieval fortress model. In reality, the lonely block happens to be stacked along with many others and together the node of buildings attracts enormous developments of infrastructure, shopping and leisure activities. Railway transport promises to introduce this model to further limits of the territory. On television, a commercial shows a running train that has the capacity to change rice fields into concrete jungles.

To alleviate the stress of the dense urban environment, each exclusive enclave is equipped with a full range of services for residents. These facilities replicate the style and organisation of a palatial hotel, offering what is dubbed 'VIP therapy'. The 24-hour services generally include baby-sitting, maid, laundry, emergency home repair, newspaper and magazine delivery, clubhouse, limousine, car park, car maintenance and shuttle-bus transport. Some of the latest developments even provide a team of doctors and tutors to more completely sever residents' interaction from the immediate urban milieu. The Belcher's brochure gently unfolds this peaceful dream:

'When your busy days draw to an end you may revel in the delights of the all-weather deluxe clubhouse and

landscaped gardens. Occupying a total area of 190,000 square feet, The Belcher's clubhouse offers all the amenities you can dream of. Sit on the deck and work on your tan. Take a dip in the 25-metre indoor swimming pool and wash away your worries. Soothe yourself in the bubble-lounge spa or Jacuzzi. Let daily pressure evaporate in the sauna. Life could not be more relaxing. If you're looking for something more invigorating, give your body a boost in the gym, unique covered tennis court, putting green or indoor multipurpose hall.'

The conflation of recreation and living places the development's clubhouse in a key position, and it articulates the transition from public podium to private apartment. Open only to members, it continues the notion of a luxury hotel as a model for mass housing – in this case for recreational sports. Detached from street level, the clubhouse sits on the roof of the podium and is designed as an outdoor theme park of recreational activities. The swimming pool is always its main feature; a landscaped garden leads to activities indoors. Inside, simulation and virtuality are often used to compensate for an evident lack of space for

such activities as skiing or golf. Through technology it is now possible to reproduce all situations. Each residential block exists as a bloated private realm where the programme of pleasures is engaged in a hostile relationship with life outside.

Further evidence of that disjunction is the e-network, which has become another key selling point for private residential buyers: 'Laguna Verde makes effective use of modern technology to make your life completely hassle-free. With our e-living service, residents have ready access to a wealth of knowledge, news and entertainment fed directly to their home through fibre optics. Our Smart card system allows easy access to the entrance lobby and car park and [can] also be used to pay your management fees. Clubhouse facilities and Lifestyle Plus services are also available through the online reservation system.'

The overall idea of the system is its unlimited capacity to provide and record data for the exclusive use of residents. The feeling of being connected certainly intensifies the belief of being one of the few fortunates, and it confirms that the private residential development is a totally controlled environment separate from the seemingly uncontrollable, high-density urban environment just outside the gates.

Above
Tsuen Kwan O housing estate plugs on to the railway station.

Opposite, left and right
Tsuen Kwan O public estate with housing and a school.

The private apartment appears as the last refuge within the massive development. It no longer matters if the dwelling space is minimal, as each habitant is free to use the entire complex as an extension of his or her personal space. As a result of the maximum optimisation of the tower plan, the 1/8 harmony cell is the minimum unit in any scheme, like eight individual houses tacked on to a central core on each floor. The logic of the plan is very simple. A typical apartment layout comprises a living/dining room, kitchen, one or two bathrooms and two or three bedrooms – all accommodated within a space measuring between 550 and 800 square feet. Circulation and other open spaces are kept to a minimum in order to maximise the efficiency of this floor area. The master bedroom is the most functional room in the apartment while the living/dining area is regarded as a showpiece. In addition to expensive materials, imported brand-name fixtures and fittings define the luxurious modern lifestyle as it is marketed.

For example, the Royal Ascot brochure clearly demonstrates the importance of floor area and finishes to the prospective buyer:

Spaciousness is a distinguishing aspect of Royal Ascot. Expansive views are complemented by gracious, uncluttered interiors. Quality fittings and finishes create an atmosphere of tranquillity and refinement. Unique architectural highlights accentuate the airy spaciousness of a more than 300-square-foot living/dining area and a master bedroom of more than 200 square feet. With an 87 per cent efficient usable floor plan, here is an environment to be savoured and filled with happy moments of harmony and delight.

The new design concept for residential tower blocks has rendered the role of the architect redundant. In order to create an illusion of 'home', developers have stretched the private boundaries of the house to absorb the public in a collective realm, but in a manner that simply repackages a standard product dating back to communist China. Moreover, that standard product perpetuates the one-child household as a model for living, and even romanticises it. Without broaching the lack of land or other issues, the private real-estate industry fulfils China's political strategy of homogeneity and collectivity versus diversity and individuality. Chic ghettos for very rich families are spreading in the urban landscape, bringing another set of battles for speculators. ⚙

In the Kingdom of the Netherlands: A Province of Architecture

Between 1993 and 2002, Amsterdam's former Eastern Docklands wharfs of Borneo and Sporenburg were redeveloped into a showcase of contemporary Dutch architecture. While entrepreneurial developers and innovative designers might deserve credit for the accomplishment, **Hans Ibelings** describes how the architectural and urban designs of Borneo and Sporenburg are also the result of a political and economic climate engineered by the government.

Zoning plans and landownership have always ensured the City of Amsterdam a dominant position in the development and realisation of building projects. In the 1990s, it exploited that position to boost architectural and urban design quality. Developers frequently make off-the-record remarks about the trouble of qualifying for projects which, they feel, place a premium on well-known architects. And while many developers are sincerely committed to architectural quality, in Amsterdam they have no choice but to aim high.

The 2,000-plus dwellings on Borneo and Sporenburg, former shipping wharfs in the Eastern Docklands area of Amsterdam, represent a high point in Dutch architecture of the 1990s. A master plan by West 8 Landscape Architects prescribed high-density, low-rise development, with an average of 100 dwellings per hectare.

The ensuing back-to-back, three-storey 'patio' dwellings represent a rich variety of architecture by an elite group of native and foreign architects that includes OMA, Enric Miralles, Claus en Kaan, Van Gameren and Mastenbroek. There are also 60 individual houses designed by, among others, MVRDV, Höhne & Rapp, Herman Hertzberger, Koen van Velsen and Gunnar Daan. The setting is punctuated by two eye-catching apartment blocks designed by Frits van Dongen and Koen van Velsen, as well

as two bright-red West 8-designed bridges, which link the residential fingers.

Borneo and Sporenburg, like the rest of the Eastern Docklands redevelopment, is a happy outcome of the Dutch polder model that rose to international prominence in the late 1990s. This consensus-based economic culture allowed city council, housing corporations and property developers to work harmoniously to create a district that is exceptionally popular with the urban middle-class. The polder model, however, is just one of several governmental stances that has made redevelopment possible, and in an architecturally distinctive fashion.

In the 1990s, the Netherlands developed into a veritable paradise of contemporary architecture. Economic prosperity and the presence of architectural talent played no small part in this, but the role of local and national government should also be stressed. In the late 1980s, the national government started to pursue a policy of promoting 'architectural quality'. The Government Buildings Agency and the Office of the Government Architect adopted this outlook, and it also prompted several of the larger municipalities, such as Amsterdam, Rotterdam, The Hague, Groningen, Maastricht, Tilburg, Zaanstad and Breda, to pay even more attention to architecture

Opening page
One of the two eccentric bridges designed by West 8, connecting the former wharfs of Sporenburg and Borneo Island.

Previous page
Aerial view of the low-rise, high-density housing on the Borneo (in front) and Sporenburg (middle) peninsulas in the Eastern Docklands of Amsterdam. Behind them is KNSM Island, built according to a master plan by Jo Coenen.

than was already the case. (Dutch architecture is much indebted to a relatively small group of aldermen and local officials, almost all of social-democratic persuasion, who championed this policy.)

That various cities have tangibly manifested architectural policy during the last decade of the 20th century is notable. The accomplishment is due to the zoning plan, which enables local governmental authorities to stipulate what may be built and where. And it is thanks to the power of possession – the government owns a lion's share of Dutch territory.

Amsterdam occupies an unusual position in the Dutch context. Apart from Rotterdam, it is the only city that owns its land, which it makes available on long (usually 50-year) leases. At the end of the leasehold period, a new ground rent is determined by the municipal development company, whose calculation is directly related to current real-estate values in accordance with the system of residual land value. For newbuild projects this is the selling price less the building costs and a margin for the developer and the contractor. Given that the value of real estate has risen much faster over the past 20 years than building costs (the last 10 years alone have seen the price of property in Amsterdam more than double), the City of Amsterdam has been able to make a tidy profit on such transactions.

Zoning plans and landownership have always ensured the City of Amsterdam a dominant position in the development and realisation of building projects. In the 1990s, it exploited that position to boost architectural and urban design quality. Developers frequently make off-the-

record remarks about the trouble of qualifying for projects which, they feel, place a premium on well-known architects. And while many developers are sincerely committed to architectural quality, in Amsterdam they have no choice but to aim high. The upshot is that outstanding plans nearly always teeter on the edge of financial infeasibility.

Just as the government formed and implemented architectural policy in the 1980s, national subsidies for public housing were abolished. The housing corporations, the traditional guardians of architectural quality, were henceforth expected to raise money for their projects themselves. They were free to build owner-occupied houses as long as they continued to fulfil their core task of providing rental housing for the less well-off.

The new dispensation cut both ways. There is a demand for private-sector dwellings, especially in Amsterdam where nearly all housing is in the subsidised rental sector (more than 80 per cent of Amsterdam's housing stock is social housing and so middle-class demand is still unsatisfied). Moreover, the returns on the sale of private dwellings made possible the construction of social-rental dwellings which, on balance, cost more than they bring in. In Amsterdam the rule of thumb is that every newbuild

Borneo, Eastern Docklands, Amsterdam

Opposite, left
Waterfront elevation of a part of the row of 60 privately developed homes on Borneo, all one-off designs by architects from Herman Hertzberger to MVRDV.

Opposite, right
End elevation of one of the rows on Borneo, designed by Dick van Gameren and Bjarne Mastenbroek, expressing the abrupt termination of the continuity of concrete tunnels, the common construction system in Dutch housing.

Below left
A super-block by Koen van Velsen, nicknamed Pacman, on Borneo, which together with the Sphinx by Frits van Dongen raised the density of this residential district from 70 units per hectare to the required level of 100 units per hectare.

Below right
One of the few exceptions to the rigidly prescribed typology (and the limited choice of materials) that the supervising designers and the municipality have allowed in the area is an extremely small corner building by Enric Miralles and Benedetta Tagliabue on Borneo.

In Amsterdam the rule of thumb is that every newbuild project should comprise 70 per cent private-sector dwellings and 30 per cent social-rental dwellings. Ostensibly, every home-buyer helps subsidise the social housing. And all of this development takes place within a rubric of architectural excellence.

Above left
Courtyard of the Sphinx on Sporenburg, with a garden by West 8, on top of an underground parking structure for 179 cars. The garden is not accessible, not even for residents of the Sphinx, for reasons of security and to reduce maintenance costs.

Above right
The Sphinx by Architecten Cie's Frits van Dongen contains 214 dwellings, 150 of which are social-rental apartments. The irregular shape of this zinc-clad building allows even the least favourably oriented units to benefit from daylight and water views.

project should comprise 70 per cent private-sector dwellings and 30 per cent social-rental dwellings. Ostensibly, every home-buyer helps subsidise the social housing. And all of this development takes place within a rubric of architectural excellence.

The Eastern Docklands redevelopment is no exception. The area, which comprises the peninsulas of Java and KNSM islands in addition to Borneo and Sporenburg, was used as wharfs until the late 1970s when the shipping industry moved westward; squatters, urban nomads, and artists filled the voids on KNSM while residual railway uses still occurred on Sporenburg. Government officials initiated redevelopment efforts in 1980, and these

plans were first executed on KNSM in 1989, then on Java. Public-private partnerships achieved the 70:30 ratio on both peninsulas, with the city, developers, investors and housing corporations assuming responsibility for different sections of the scheme. The Construction Industry Social Fund (SFB) was the main player in the Java Island development, for example.

Nowhere was the partnership so complex and the interests so entwined as on Borneo and Sporenburg, where two-thirds of the development was produced by an ad-hoc development company called New Deal. New Deal, along with the city council and the municipal development company, commissioned the spatial master plan of the two islands. This master plan was drawn up by West 8 Landscape Architects, with input from three local officials: Jan de Waal of the Housing Service, Ton Schaap of the Urban Planning Service and Jurgen Bos of the city's Project Management Department.

New Deal was made up of three Amsterdam housing corporations – Eigen Haard, De Doelen and Onze Woning (the last two merged, during the development of Borneo and Sporenburg, with Woonstichting De Key) – and three contractors/developers: MUWI, Intervam and Moes. They built 1,450 dwellings, mostly on Sporenburg (90 per cent of Sporenburg was developed by New Deal). One-third of the dwellings are social housing which, upon completion, became the property of one of the housing corporations involved. The remaining 600 dwellings are mainly private-sector rental and owner-occupied housing and were developed by Casa (property developer), the SFB (investor), Smits and De Nijs (construction companies) and De Principaal (developer for De Key housing corporation).

The final piece of the whole development and New Deal's crowning glory was to have been the Fountainhead apartment block, the district's third, to be designed by Steven Holl.

However, because Holl withdrew, Dutch co-architect Kees Christiaanse completed the design. Owing to the recent collapse in demand, the building, containing apartments of a luxury (and price) unheard of in Amsterdam, was cancelled in May 2003, a temporary playground taking its place.

Even without this final project, Borneo and Sporenburg are in many respects a success. The area is popular with residents and for several years now has attracted a steady stream of architectural tourists. West 8's master plan has been executed in strict accordance with the rules laying down a 3.5-metre ceiling height on the ground floor, a sharp separation between street and private domain and a restriction of facade materials to dark-red brick and Oregon pine frames. This lends the district a great sense of unity, if occasional monotony. Further variation was reduced at the behest of the developers. Because they considered a lot of small projects consisting of four or eight dwellings to be financially infeasible, the district now consists mostly of larger units.

Variation abounds, however, in the row of 60 private development plots on Borneo where individuals were permitted to build a home of their own, designed by an architect of their choice (but approved by a supervisory team). These houses are now trotted out ad nauseam by proponents of private home-building; for example, the former junior minister for Housing, Spatial Planning and the Environment proclaimed that by 2005 one-third of all new housing in urban development areas should be built by the prospective residents. In a country with virtually no tradition of self-building and where local authorities hold all the trump cards, this sounds like a pretty unrealistic goal – not least because there is no municipality in the Netherlands where private individuals can easily purchase a building plot. △

Below left and right
South elevation of a housing project on Borneo by Arne van Herk and Sabien de Kleijn. It comprises patio houses with wedge-shaped floor plans on the lower levels, with apartments and duplexes on the top.

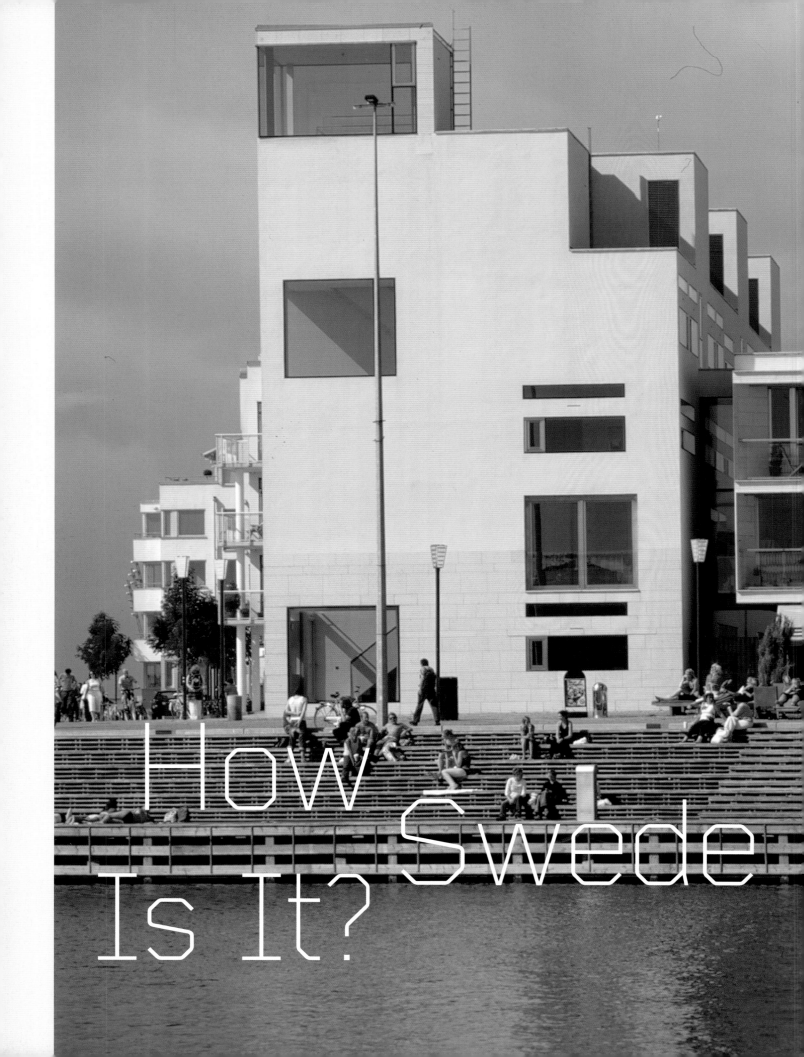

The sun of a new decade shone down on my head. A whole new city of steel, glass and concrete stood on what had been an empty plane. Houses, restaurants and music stands looked like birds, lifting on stiff wings.[1]

This is how Ivar Lo-Johansson, a distinguished mid-century Swedish writer, recalled his visit to the 1930 Stockholm Exhibition where the architecture, he continued, 'marked the birth of a new frame of mind'. Since the introduction of Scandinavian Modernism at this exhibition, housing exhibitions have become a Swedish tradition. Each attempts to replicate the Stockholm Exhibition's success and perhaps the most fruitful of these efforts took place in 1955 in the southern city of Helsingborg; indeed, H55 is regarded as an important benchmark for Scandinavian design. Over the last few decades, different Swedish cities have attempted similar exhibitions, mostly to inaugurate new neighbourhoods and market their cities.

Bo01 in Malmö, Sweden's third largest city, is a recent example. Located in the Western Harbour, a former industrial area about a 25-minute walk from the city centre, Bo01 is a housing exhibition with a specific strategic mission: to promote a city that has undergone tremendous changes since the 1970s. After the decline of its industry – mostly shipbuilding – a new economy based on education, technology and culture has dramatically reshaped the image of Malmö. In the summer of 2001 the exhibition, with a main focus on ecology and new technology, became one of the city's tools to project a new image of itself and to market the post-industrial district as a rewarding place to live and work (the 'Bo' in Bo01 is Swedish for 'live').

Bo01 presented a plethora of temporary exhibitions, experimental gardens and art shows, as well as a permanent residential neighbourhood facing the ocean and the new bridge that links Malmö to Copenhagen. Apart from its 'green' design standards, diversity is perhaps the most significant keyword to describe this new neighbourhood. The great variety of housing types – apartments and terrace houses, rentals and co-ops – displays a wide range of shapes, materials and colours. Much attention is given to public space: parks, canals, bridges and inner courtyards protected from strong winds. The café-lined promenade acts as a continuation of the adjacent broad beaches.

Klas Tham is the exhibition architect and author of Bo01's plan. A designer of dull, uniform slabs for the official Swedish housing programme of 35 years ago, Tham, like many other architects of his generation, has since turned in the opposite direction. He is now a proponent of Dionysian disorder, diversity and multiplicity. Tham says that his childhood fishing village is a source of inspiration for Bo01, but so is the scale and density of the medieval northern European city.

As **Patrick Amsellem** relates, Bo01 represents the most architecturally ambitious building construction to take place in the Swedish city of Malmö since the dissolution of public housing policy in the 1960s. But this new model of public–private collaboration may have resulted in more architectural eclecticism than integrated vision for the future.

Opposite
Outdoor life along the promenade, next to Gert Wingårdh's rental apartment building, where 11 of the 23 flats extend over two or more floors.

Above
Bo01, Malmö, Sweden, 2001
A combination of local energy sources such as wind power, solar energy and heat pumps makes Bo01 self-sufficient. In Månsson Dahlbäck's 'Brick Castle', solar panels on the roof and on the southern wall become part of the architectural expression.

'A web structure for the city district,' Tham says, 'has confirmed its value and capacity to support urban life for thousands of years.' Apart from the emphasis on renewable materials, shelter, vegetation and the priority for pedestrian and bicycle traffic, Tham points to 'mystery, surprise, possibilities of getting lost and making accidental discoveries' as crucial aspects of the plan.[2]

Conditions for Development

Private and public co-operation has a long tradition in Swedish housing, but the conditions have changed over the years. Sweden can no longer afford the strong policy of public funding, subsidies and beneficial loans that fuelled the progressive projects of the 1930s, 1940s and 1950s and the bureaucratic mass solutions of the 1960s. As policy was abandoned in the last two decades, so was construction. The private sector is the motor behind nearly all construction, but because rents, with few exceptions, are still more or less regulated, developers have no way of getting their money back from building rental property.

One of the architects at Testbedstudio, an office that designed two temporary pavilions for Bo01, Jonas Olsson says of many properties for sale: 'The large developers, often stock

companies, never jeopardise their situation. There is a lack of the kind of openness and curiosity that leads to the magnificent and provoking results that you see in countries like Holland. In Sweden the market determines what will be built and the companies don't build unless the property is already sold. That's why most things built here today are orderly and grey – it all looks the same.'

In the current Swedish construction climate, Bo01 suggests a very different solution in terms of organisation and initiative. The city rather than private developers was the primary driving force.

Bo01 was a wholly owned subsidiary of Svensk Bostadsmässa (Swedish Housing Exhibition), founded in 1987 by the Swedish housing department with a number of Swedish cities as co-owners. Its aim was to stimulate the debate on housing, architecture and technology. Originally planned for another site in the summer of 2000, the Malmö exhibition was deferred one year because of organisational difficulties. It was renamed Bo01 and as its location was moved to the Western Harbour, city officials assumed most responsibility for the project.

The exhibition, with its new permanent neighbourhood, could now be integrated with the city's master plan for the entire old harbour in order to transform it into a complete district for living, working and studying. (The recently founded University of Malmö was already located in the area.) According to Malmö's structural plan, the district should have the character

Bo01, Malmö, Sweden, 2001
The taller houses lining the promenade create the impression of a city wall, and the use of narrow alleyways increases the feeling of moving through a village.

of an inner city. Tham was employed by Bo01 to design the detailed plan for the exhibition's part of the area. The city was the largest landowner and it also retained the right to finalise the plan.

Malmö was allocated 250 million SEK by the federal government through a local investment programme to support the environmentalist ambitions of the new neighbourhood. It was the developers who took the main economic risks of building houses without further subsidies. Nevertheless, the developers were required to participate and collaborate in an unusual collective process: before the city sold the land, a dialogue between developers, architects, planners and city officials resulted in guidelines for shaping the exhibition and the new neighbourhood. The goal of the programme was to give the developers a common platform and an operative tool that would secure the high ambitions set up by Bo01 and the city regarding ecology, technology and architectural design.

'Even though the developers negotiated for a vaguer programme than was initially intended,' says Eva Dalman, the area architect for Bo01 at the Malmö City Planning Office, 'I'm really impressed that so much of the contents were finally realised, especially in terms of ecology and renewable energy.' Dalman was closely involved in supervising the guidelines as well as the neighbourhood's ecological sustainability as a whole, and says that currently 100 per cent of the energy consumption at Bo01 is renewable.

A small-scale division of property was an important and unusual move to secure Tham's vision of architectural diversity and multiplicity at Bo01. Small blocks were divided into individual plots which allowed the involvement of smaller developers and construction companies in collaboration with different architects. Even though the developers were ultimately responsible for the architectural design of the projects, Bo01 was influential in the coupling of architects and developers. The guidelines stated that Bo01 and the city had to accept the architects chosen by the developers, and Tham also produced a hotly debated list of qualified architects. When possible, Bo01 tried to find good matches between developers and architects. Regardless of the difficulties caused by time constraints, there is a general consensus that the collaboration between the real-estate community and the architects went relatively well. In most cases the architects were allowed much autonomy.

Criticism and Response
Despite this freedom, the critical reactions to the built environment have been mixed. Whereas the public spaces are generally praised for the successful landscaping, the architecture is often discounted as boring and uninspiring. There was also a widespread

Bo01, Malmö, Sweden, 2001

belief that the outcome is unnecessarily heterogeneous. 'When there are no real guidelines for the design and no time for the architects to react on what the neighbours are up to, the resulting clash becomes superficial – a mishmash with no correlation between the buildings,' Olsson says. The wide-ranging variations are undoubtedly part of Tham's idea of diversity, but it takes time to create the sensation of a community that has been allowed to grow organically.

The main problem, however, is that freedom failed to bring more innovative and creative solutions. With the exception of Gert Wingårdh's apartment building – a beautiful, unconventional block of flats in stainless steel, glass and stone (which, interestingly enough, was built by the city-owned developer MKB) – and a few other designs that try to break with a conventional sense of domesticity, most projects are safe and predictable. The Neo-Modernism that has been the dominant fashion in Swedish architecture since the 1990s also prevails at Bo01. Even though many interior spaces are of high quality, more unconventional and experimental solutions might have been expected from an exhibition that wished to show housing of the future.

Only a few blocks away from Bo01 is the impressive Ribershus, built in the 1930s and for a long time considered the most modern of Swedish buildings. An example of the new architecture developed in the wake of the Stockholm Exhibition, this huge apartment house introduced new ways of handling domestic space and modified the concept of living in the 1930s and 1940s.

Apart from its ecological ambitions, this might be what Bo01 ultimately lacks: a vision, a sense of new possibilities and a willingness to really experiment. Again, most of the blame falls on the conservative Swedish building industry, which invests in a conventional vision of the future rather than taking a risk in trying out provocative and unorthodox concepts.

It was in the temporary exhibitions and in the contributions to the various competitions launched by Bo01 that the most interesting and vital ideas were produced. But many of the temporary projects were cancelled, such as the 'Future Homes – From Earth to Mars and Back Again' show, planned in collaboration with NASA. And the competitions were often a source of discontent between architects and developers, mainly because no developer was prepared to realise the prize-winning ideas. Although Malmö-based Sesam won a competition for innovative wood interiors, principal Ola Månsson says: 'We were told to do the fund-raising for the project ourselves.' Again, the competition had not involved the developers, even though it was their apartments that were to be adapted for the winning solutions. 'When we finally found someone willing to do the interior, the developer had already finalised the plans. The walls were built and the compromises we had to do rendered the original idea impossible.'

At Bo01 there will be no contemporary equivalent to Ivar Lo-Johansson, who 'walked about looking for the

New Human Being' at the Stockholm Exhibition in 1930. But despite its many problems and conventional solutions, the new neighbourhood has proved to be popular. In March of this year, 78 per cent of all property at Bo01 was sold or rented; of a total of 557 apartments, 289 are co-ops and the remaining 268 are rentals, of which 197 are student housing for the nearby university. Most of the apartments that remain empty are large and very expensive, and those involved admit that they miscalculated the market. 'Nobody realised that it would be so expensive,' Dalman says, 'we were too busy focusing on the ecological sustainability.' (The hurried construction time was also an important reason why Bo01 turned out to be so expensive.)

Many critics have condemned the new neighbourhood as an isolated enclave for the wealthy, especially because the city is already segregated and houses a huge immigrant population. But after the summer of 2002, it became clear that the neighbourhood's promenade, parks and many restaurants and cafés have become destinations also for people from less privileged parts of the city.

Still, Jesper Meijling, a critic and early commentator, thinks that the plan lacks urban qualities: 'Bo01 turns away from its context and from the city,' Meijling says. 'The neighbourhood feels like a dense and narrow village and it exemplifies old-school thinking that ignores urban discussions of the past 20

Notes
1 Eva Rudberg, *Stockholm Exhibition 1930: Modernism's Breakthrough in Swedish Architecture*, Stockholmia (Stockholm), 1999, trans Paul Britten Austin and Frances Lucas.
2 *Bo01 – Staden: Byggnaderna, planen, processen, håkkbargeten*, AB Svensk Byggtjänst (Stockholm), 2001.

years.' He points out that Bo01 is detached from the rest of the area and, more importantly, from the industrial past of the harbour district where it is located. 'The planning,' he says, 'is not strategic and it doesn't allow for any economic processes to ever start here.' Meijling and many other observers acknowledge the ultimately positive impact of Bo01 on Malmö, but many see the plan's lack of site specificity as its most important disadvantage. Instead of using a country village as a model, Meijling believes that Bo01 could have been a more interesting project had it operated within different sections of the entire Western Harbour: 'It could have included broader activities, a theatre for example, and thus used different means to initiate urban processes.'

Even if the current construction of Santiago Calatrava's sculptural apartment building, Turning Torso, hardly promises to provide low-income housing in the Western Harbour, the price level at Bo01 made the city acutely aware of the importance of cheaper housing in the area. It is currently planning a land-use competition where developers and architects will suggest ways to residentially develop the area with high-quality low-income housing. Moreover, the experience gained from Bo01 and the development of the university is now being used to connect the old port with the city centre and to transform the entire Western Harbour into a mixed urban environment with workplaces, shops, restaurants and places to live. Two years after Bo01, it certainly seems as if the city of Malmö has begun listening to its critics with a keen ear. ⚷

Patrick Amsellem is a Swedish-born critic based in New York City, where he writes for Swedish magazines and newspapers. He is currently a PhD candidate in architectural history and art history at the Institute of Fine Arts, New York University.

Helen Castle is editor of *Architectural Design* and executive commissioning editor of Wiley-Academy.

Laurent Gutierrez and Valérie Portefaix are French architects who live and work in Hong Kong. In 1997 they founded MAP Office, a collaborative studio that incorporates architecture and the visual arts. They have participated in several local and international exhibitions, including the 7th Architecture Venice Biennale. Among their several publications are *Mapping HK* (2000), which details both the physical and dynamic transformations taking place in Hong Kong, and *HK LAB* (2002), in which Hong Kong is seen as an advance laboratory for innovative solutions.

Art historian Hans Ibelings is an independent architecture critic. His publications include *Twentieth Century Architecture in the Netherlands* (1995), *Supermodernism: Architecture in the Age of Globalization* (1998/enlarged edition 2003), *The Artificial Landscape: Contemporary Architecture, Urbanism and Landscape Architecture in The Netherlands* (2000) and monographs on Dutch architects *Meyer & Van Schooten* (2001) and *Claus en Kaan* (2001). His most recent book is on Meyer & Van Schooten's ING House in Amsterdam, published in spring 2003.

As principal-in-charge of design at Jones Studio, Eddie Jones has received numerous local, national and international design commendations. He studied at Oklahoma State University and has 32 years' experience designing public- and private-sector projects. His experience with the Arizona Native American population has provided him with the unique opportunity to study the historic precedents of indigenous desert architecture. He regularly lectures and presents the firm's work to various colleges, universities and institutions around the world.

Jeremy Melvin is a writer who specialises in architecture. He is a contributing editor to *Architectural Design* and has contributed to many professional, national and international publications. He studied architecture and history of architecture at the Bartlett, UCL, and teaches history of architecture at South Bank University, London, as well as being a consultant to the Royal Academy's architecture programme.

Jayne Merkel is a contributing editor to *Architectural Design* and was for many years editor of *Oculus*, the journal for the New York Chapter of the AIA. Also an art historian and architecture critic, she has written about art for *Artforum* and about architecture for *Art in America* and other publications. She has worked as a curator at several museums and has taught art history and criticism at the Rhode Island School of Design, Parsons School of Design, Miami University and the Art Academy of Cincinnati.

Aimee Molloy, a New York-based freelance writer, received her masters degree in urban planning from NYU and writes mainly on topics associated with planning and design. As director of exhibitions and programmes for the Municipal Art Society of New York, she handles the advocacy group's curatorial responsibilities. Her articles have appeared in *Icon* as well as *City Limits*.

Sara Moss, a former assistant editor at *Architecture* magazine, studied at Columbia University where she earned a master's degree in architecture. She lives in New York and writes about, photographs and draws construction. She has contributed design commentary to National Public Radio and several of her photographs and illustrations were published by the Van Alen Institute to accompany its exhibition 'Renewing, Rebuilding, Remembering'.

David B Sokol is managing editor of *I.D.* magazine and guest-editor of this issue of *Architectural Design*. He has been a regular contributor to *Architecture*, *Metropolis* and *Architectural Record* magazines. His most recent essay for *Architectural Design* was 'Come out, Join in, Get off', an examination of interior design in the club environments of New York gay subculture.

A regular contributor to *Architectural Design*, Masaaki Takahashi is a Tokyo-based freelance journalist who has written about design, architecture and culture for numerous Japanese and UK magazines. He regularly explores the consequences of the Japanese building boom, as well as its representation in the mass media. He has studied art and design in both Europe and the US.

Leon van Schaik is innovation professor of architecture at the Royal Melbourne Institute of Technology (RMIT). He works internationally with practitioners who have established mastery in their field, engaging them in critical review of the nature of their mastery, its enabling structures, its knowledge bases and the implications of the nexus between these for emerging forms of research-led practice. His latest book is *The Practice of Practice: Research in the Medium of Design* (RMIT Press, Melbourne, 2003).

Stephen Varady is an architect and director of Stephen Varady Architecture, an innovative practice exploring alternative ideas for residential, commercial and hypothetical projects. He has been a lecturer and design teacher since 1984 in architecture schools in Sydney, Newcastle and Melbourne, and is also an architecture critic, writer and photographer with work published in Australia, the UK, Germany, Spain and the US, in magazines including *Architecture Australia*, *Monument*, *World Architecture*, *Architecture Review* and *Architectural Design*.

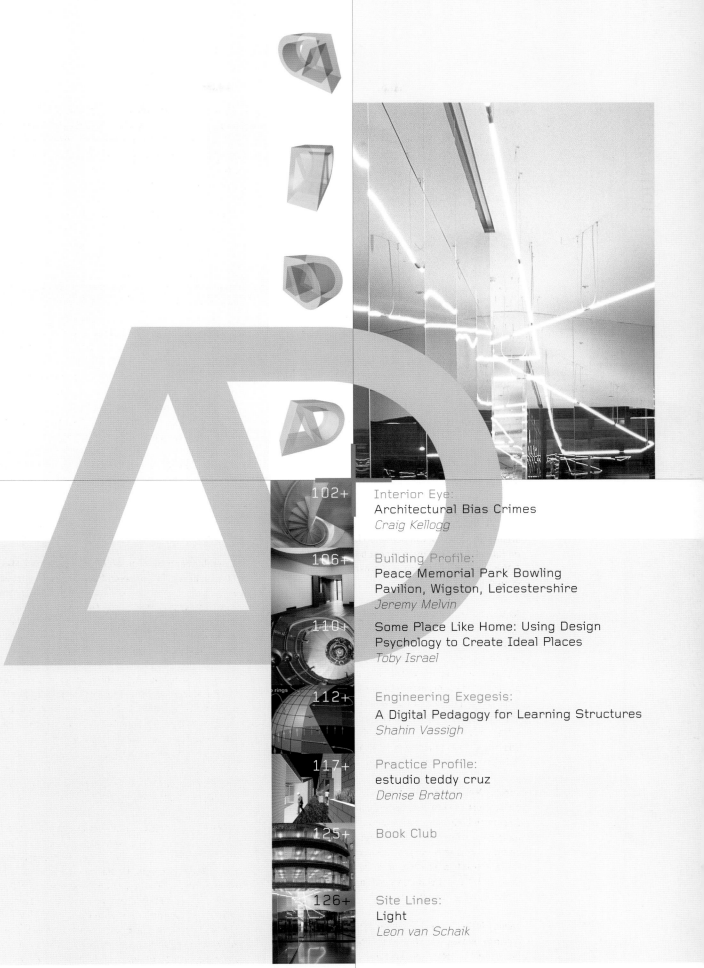

Architectural Bias Crimes

Both logistics and aesthetics limit architectural interiors in print. **Craig Kellogg** exposes a few of the many obstacles interiors face in finding their largest possible audience.

Manhattan's Austrian Cultural Forum, a hotly anticipated 24-storey tower in New York by the cult architect Raimund Abraham, made a brisk and promising debut in *Wallpaper** magazine in 2002. I should know: I placed that piece and wrote it, too. On to a single page we crammed four indelible views of Abraham's iconic facade, which he admits resembles a guillotine. Views not shown were, however, just as interesting. We had none of the Forum director's private office, with its quartet of armchairs in tubular chrome. There was no picture of the grand piano on a cantilevered platform in the Forum's auditorium; nothing of that platform riding up into a notch in the ceiling, along a track hidden in the sidewall of the stage. And we didn't show the director's private apartment on the tower's top floors, which are linked by a wooden spiral stairway as trim as a Chinese puzzle.

I used every scrap available for the *Wallpaper** story on the building's facades and interiors concept. Presumably we weren't allowed any interiors photos at that early stage because the publicist wanted to save them for editors who would follow when the real-estate reality on the site finally caught up with publishers' schedules. But, as the months progressed, a lot of what ran elsewhere concerned the guillotine, with barely a hint of the piano or spiral stairs. The architecture critic for *New York* magazine, Joseph Giovannini, produced a review accompanied by one smallish image of the facade, as did *Time Out New York*. (Quite possibly, it was the same picture.) The *Financial Times* and the *New Yorker* both printed singular images that showed the building in profile, to highlight the nose-like projection on the street facade.

Towards the end of April, the *New York Times* supplied what must have been the first glimpse inside: three disconnected interior views. But for a thoroughgoing introduction to the whole building, where interiors lingered incomplete many months after the facade, it was necessary to wait for the June issue of *Architecture* magazine or *Architectural Record* in August. Unfortunately, by that point the popular media had moved on to newer news. So most people with no business in the building today judge it as a facade and nothing more. This is a shame, as the audaciously kinetic piano platform in the auditorium is, for a start, a bravado gesture unlike any elsewhere in New York.

Interiors such as Abraham's, which function on a conceptual plane, challenge conventional architectural wisdom; the idea persists that interiors are 'lite' when compared with facades. Of course, this is an old-fashioned attitude and architects have largely abandoned it. However, the fact remains that interiors

are generally more ephemeral. We expect them to evolve in a way facades do not, and we honour them less as a result.

This is among a constellation of contributing factors in what I have come to see as an exteriors bias in American publishing. Photography probably plays the most obvious role in perpetuating the imbalance. Editors will short-change coverage if they find themselves working with a limited supply of suitable interiors pictures. According to Sarah Amelar, a senior editor at *Architectural Record*: 'Sometimes interiors get short shrift in the shoot of an entire building.'

And it would seem that interiors themselves – even showy interesting examples by notable architects – occasionally share the blame for poor pictures. Abraham won the commission for the Forum tower based on his layouts which, although tight, make the

Clockwise, from top left
Interior stairs link levels in the double-height library. A skylight offers a towering view of the rear facade. The skylight illuminates the stair landing that floats above a basement gallery. Tubular chrome chairs occupy the director's office alcove, which projects from the mask-like street facade as a nose.

Bluestone paves the stair landing, which is edged with glass plates. The same flooring is used on the roof, for a covered party terrace that opens to city views through an unglazed trapezoidal void.

best of a minuscule floor plate. Amelar offers a general comment on the way New York buildings, with their small rooms, can rankle photographers: 'It can be tricky to get back far enough and find the right angles to really capture a space.' Equally, lighting is almost always more challenging indoors than out.

Any imbalance in the coverage of interiors in the architectural press today has historic precedents. Mildred Schmertz, who capped 33 years at *Architectural Record* by serving as the magazine's editor in chief, explains that advertising once came mostly from suppliers of building products, not furniture: 'We weren't in the business of focusing on interior design,' she says. *Architectural Record* 'gradually increased its coverage of interiors simply because architects were doing more of them,' she adds. Younger architects eventually began using interior design to make their reputations. And soon enough, designers 'discovered

that they could make more money doing interiors than doing buildings'.

This partly explains the steady supply of notable interiors currently featured in the architectural press. Indeed, *Architectural Record* was among the publications that supported the broad coverage of interiors at the Austrian Cultural Forum for an audience of professional designers. The popular press, however, lags behind. Granted, the popular magazines supply a steady diet of extraordinary residential interiors for lay readers. But consumer magazines offer relatively little on restaurants, churches, schools, shops or concert halls with interiors by architects. In collaboration with interiors photographers, it's time for the general-interest magazines in America to begin granting the attention and analysis that architectural interiors deserve. △

Below
The drum has a robust finish, but features such as the bandstand allow it to engage with the park.

Opposite top left
Site plan. The position and proportions of the bowling green were fixed: what Patel Taylor tried

to do was to use geometry and form to offset its impact in the park and to make the new building address all directions.

Opposite bottom left
Ground plan. In planning a circular building, Patel Taylor adopted a *poche* approach, as if the main central space is carved from a solid volume. This gives it some

Peace Memorial Park
Bowling Pavilion
Wigston, Leicestershire

Jeremy Melvin describes how an 'elegant and deceptively simple' design for a bowling pavilion has helped regenerate a village on the edge of Leicester, shifting local attitudes and the community's perceptions of its 19th-century park.

privacy, though the entrance, bandstand, oriel window and rooflight break through to the outside. It also makes for a logical disposition of spaces, with male and female changing rooms and WCs on either side, with a servery/kitchen taking the last arc.

Below top right
Exploded axonometric, showing (from bottom) the base elements (hedges, bandstand, columns etc), the space enclosures (drum and canopy) and the interior.

Below bottom right
Section. The drum structure is simple: concrete slab, blockwork walls and concrete roof. The canopy is a steel frame with cedar slats, marked by dramatic cantilevers.

Once a local authority spots a piece of leftover land, the probability is that it will designate it a 'park', plant a few trees, put in a few benches, maybe cut the grass once in a while and leave the rest to chance. What happens then is a wonderful maelstrom of atavistic competition between classes, generations and interest groups that would leave students of sociology gasping for breath at the semiritualised, demi-licensed conflicts. How to change these perceptions and capitalise on the potential they offer is the sort of thing the think-tank Demos writes pamphlets about. But that typical history, more or less emblematically, was the story of the Peace Memorial Park in Wigston, a village on the outskirts of Leicester, for its first 75 years, before consultants Park Life asked Patel Taylor to come up with a quick design to replace the bowling pavilion as the centrepiece of an application for a Heritage Lottery Fund grant back in 1995.

The park evolved through accident and opportunism rather than conscious design and decision. In the aftermath of the First World War acquiring a memorial of some sort must have seemed a necessity, but grief, however powerful, does not segue naturally into a sustainable public facility. Shortly after being acquired for this purpose in the early 1920s, the local bowling club moved in and placed the unforgivingly rigid geometry of its green almost in the centre of the park, taking up a large chunk of the 2-acre space and dividing the residual areas from each other. In 1928 it built a pavilion overlooking the green and turning its back to the other areas, reinforcing the sense they had of being backland, sandwiched between the bare side of a barn-like Congregational chapel and the rear of a terrace of houses. Sometime afterwards the equally prescribed yet smaller form of a tennis court took shape alongside the bowling green and the local vandals began a long, though intermittent, siege of the increasingly ghettoised bowlers. The bowlers responded with periodic pavilion extensions and this remained the cycle until the National Heritage Memorial Fund decided to devote much of its money from the National Lottery to urban parks.

Patel Taylor quickly realised that it would have to bring a degree of conscious form-making to unify the various accidents and ciphers which had previously defined the park. The basic design comprising a solid squat drum with a light wispy canopy, the ethereal qualities of which are reinforced by its dappled shadows and long cantilevers, emerged fairly quickly in direct response to the need to offset the green's rigid geometry and mediate

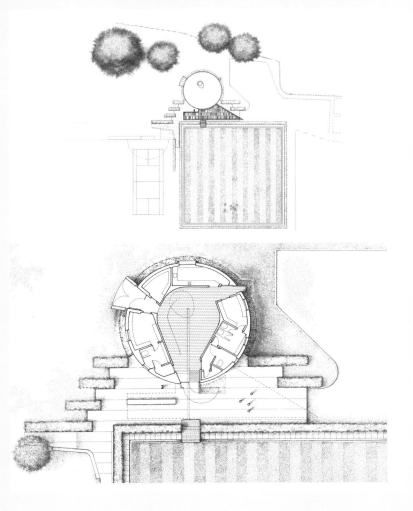

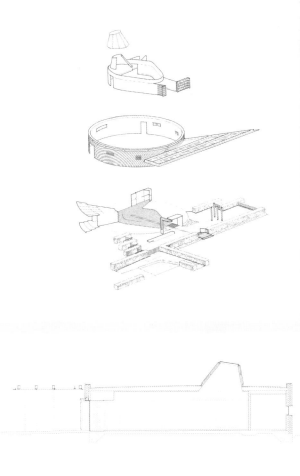

Top right
The canopy frames views across the green.

Bottom left
If the square bowling green and circular pavilion both have geometries that suggest exclusion, the light floating canopy mediates between them and, with its elegance and intrigue, lures people inwards.

Bottom right
The bowling club members are not unduly troubled with assertive Modernism, rather a gentle background to their slow-paced sport. The church tower is just out of the picture to the right.

between it and the rest of the park. Its form is deliberately omnidirectional, though the canopy, the prime function of which is to provide a shady spot for watching bowls, also adds a parallax that makes the view from every angle unique, and the irregularly placed group of four columns, supporting a precariously long cantilever, reinforces this effect. The pavilion is deliberately set to one side of the green so as to introduce another organising axis, and at one point a smaller canopy breaks through the timber cladding to provide a small bandstand facing away from the tennis courts and bowling green.

So much for its practical and functional qualities: like all good designs, this particular composition engages in a series of dialogic relationships with its location and site. On its own a drum would probably seem defensive and exclusive, though the canopy is an enticing and welcoming feature in the heart of the park. From the far end of the bowling green it underlines a view of the fine Decorated tower of St Wystan's Church, a reminder that Wigston's origins date back to the sixth century and that it has a distinctive form which WG Hoskins, the historian at Leicester University who pioneered the study of landscape as a historic artefact, considered one of the clearest examples of a 'ring fence' village, where buildings formed the defensive perimeter of an enclosed space. Traces of this layout remain: St Wystan's marks one corner of the enclosure and the Peace Memorial Park lies more or less at its middle, the paths through it following something akin to the systems of lanes that gave access to individually cultivated 'strips'. And this plan form was as rigid, and depended as much on non-aesthetic prescriptions, as the regulations for sports grounds. Over time, other uses evolved: a plague pit lies nearby and the local gaol once stood on the site of the park.

Below left
A dramatic rooflight lights the main interior space.

Below right
Providing a shady spot for spectators was part of the brief: Patel Taylor turned this into a
subtle interplay of light, structure and form.

To capitalise on these tantalising threads, Patel Taylor had to develop the design once the lottery application was successful, though the initial challenge, remembers Pankaj Patel, was to devise an effective plan for a circular building. Fortunately the brief was fairly simple – for a main meeting room served by a kitchen, as well as ancillary facilities including ones for people with disabilities. The result is elegant and deceptively simple. A teardrop-shaped room occupies the centre of the plan, as if hollowed from a solid volume, the residue of which contains changing rooms – male one side, female the other – kitchen and store. It breaks through the enclosure at four points: the entrance door facing the green, an oriel slit window, the bandstand and a copper-clad lantern which projects above the roof. While not completely detached from the outside the pavilion has a sense of isolation which probably helps to keep the rivalries of the bowling green away from the social functions, and also makes it suitable for use as a day nursery. Its oak floor and gentle light are worlds away from most small-scale sports pavilions.

As the pavilion achieves its effects through careful detailing, the basic construction is simple. Blockwork walls rest on a concrete slab; the roof is also concrete with steel trimmings, while the canopy is steel-framed. What gives the building its rich texture is the horizontally banded cedar cladding, and the cedar lattice on the canopy. Through this certain events, like the eruption of the rooflight and other windows, suggest connections between inside and out. The pavilion design established a language for other interventions in the park, largely in steel with cedar boarding.

One of the central aims of the pavilion was to change perceptions of the park, and such a goal needs a hiatus of some sort, something to break the cycle. So much is common to many urban parks, but at Wigston the need is particularly acute. Its deeply inscribed physical form is that of a village, while its proximity to Leicester imports the social patterns of a large city, among them vandalism.

In a traditional village powerful social patterns are often closely interwoven with physical ones, limiting the scope for architectural expression, while in a city, as erudite urban commentators keep telling us, architecture is irrelevant compared to the fast-moving signs and economic undercurrents. But under these circumstances it may be that where village and city meet is one point where architecture has potential. On Pevsner's old bicycle-shed-Lincoln-Cathedral principle, architecture introduces a degree of conscious manipulation into the ongoing processes that create our environment. Patel Taylor's pavilion makes its forms and functions explicit so that they rise into the realm of consciousness. There is no naive functionalist hope that the right building will induce the right behaviour, nor a suggestion that the design is a prototype for pavilions everywhere. Rather there is a sense that the pavilion encourages a measure of contemplation and speculation by the way it engages with the rich palimpsest of its physical context. This is something that no local authority dictate could do, though it is a necessary start in the process of changing perceptions. ⟰

Left
The stockyard pens of Michael Graves's boyhood.

Right
Graves's sketch of the original plan for his present
warehouse residence.

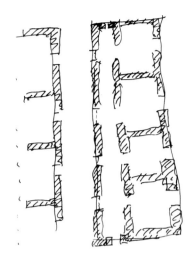

Some Place Like Home:
Using Design Psychology to create Ideal Places

Would you believe an author who claims to have written a book that challenges
our most basic notions of home, of place and, ultimately, of architecture and
design? We might pause and swivel around in our chairs but, before doing a
360-degree turn and rethinking all assumptions about our profession, we would
want to read *Some Place Like Home: Using Design Psychology to Create Ideal
Places* by Toby Israel. In this book, startling interviews conducted with design-
world superstars Michael Graves, Andres Duany and Charles Jencks reveal
how their 'environmental autobiographies' — their past histories of place —
unconsciously influenced their choice of home, their well-known public projects
and their widely influential philosophies.

These are not typical 'tell me about your projects and work'
interviews. Instead they are based on a carefully developed
series of 'design psychology' exercises administered to Graves,
Duany and Jencks to encourage them to recall their past,
present and future senses of place and home.

Through the magnifying glass of memory, the author helped
the designers recollect the houses, rooms, back yards, streets
and neighbourhoods that hold deep personal meaning for each
of them. This heightened their awareness of the ways in which
these early experiences impacted their later lives as they have
reworked, replicated or rejected (often unconsciously) their
past environmental experiences.

For example, Graves remembered a favourite transcendent
childhood place — the stockyards where his father worked:

'An exaggerated building with great, elevated
passageways all made of wood, which crisscrossed
in the air … It was not just the passageways, but
that you looked down on the animals in their pens.'
Interestingly, Graves's current home in Princeton,
New Jersey, a ruin when he found it, was originally
a furniture warehouse. The book's astounding
comparison photographs illustrate how the warehouse's
floor plan, originally divided into 44 long thin rooms,
echoed the same form as the stockyards of Graves's
childhood. Israel suggests that the internal form of
the warehouse, packaged in the Italianate ruin-like
wrapping Graves fell in love with during time spent in
Italy in his twenties, may have been the driving (though

subconscious) force behind his attraction to the New Jersey building he now calls home.

The author continues to build her case by illustrating how places from the past contain the seeds of Duany's and Jencks's future choices for their private homes and, most importantly, of the ground-breaking design trends they have championed. In a moment of epiphany, after completing an 'environmental family tree' exercise, Duany realised the link between his grandparents' courtyard home and the courtyard homes he designs into his New Urbanist communities which now proliferate across the US.

Grandparents' houses seem to loom large in the environmental story of all three designers.[1] Charles Jencks was intrigued by the suggestion that his grandmother's house was not only the key to the home he designed for himself, but also reverberated in the architectural theory he has developed throughout his career. He commented that the book's author was creating 'a new paradigm in architecture' of interest to architects around the world.

In fact, *Some Place Like Home* announces the founding of a whole new 'inner vision' field of design psychology defined as 'the practice of architecture, planning and interior design in which psychology is the principal design tool'. The purpose of design psychology is to create environments that not only reflect the individual or group but support and encourage positive change in the whole person or organisation.

Israel, originally trained as an environmental psychologist, explains how well-established fascinating theory and research in this area can be practically applied offering, as Duany realised, 'a great deal of efficiency focusing the

client'. The last portion of the book includes examples of residential, corporate and institutional projects created via the design psychology process. A 'design psychology toolbox' at the end gives professionals hands-on programming exercises they can use 'to explore and design from the client's most fulfilling inner experiences'. Thus the book shows how both 'inner vision' and programme requirements can be translated in a ground-breaking way into compelling design.

By now, you may be leaning back in your chair remembering your own environmental family tree and wondering how it has influenced your choice of places. By lacing her own poetic housing-hunting story throughout the book, Israel engages readers in an intimate, personal way, inviting them to do the exercises themselves so that they can 'read the poetry that is their space, in order to create some place that truly feels like home'. ◬

Note
1 As Dr Constance Forrest of Forrest/Painter Design has observed, it may be that grandparents' houses are an oasis providing respite for harried parents and relaxed, unconditional love for the child from doting grandparents.

If you enjoyed reading this article, then you might be interested in purchasing *Some Place Like Home* by Toby Israel (ISBN 0470849509), available to ◬ readers for an exclusive price of £16.95 (over 30% off rrp). All you have to do is quote the code CKX when you order directly through John Wiley & Sons Ltd, and you will receive the book at the special price (+p&p). Offer ends 31 March 2004. Order using any of the methods listed at the back of this issue or by visiting www.wileyeurope.com, ensuring that you quote the promotion code to take advantage of this offer.

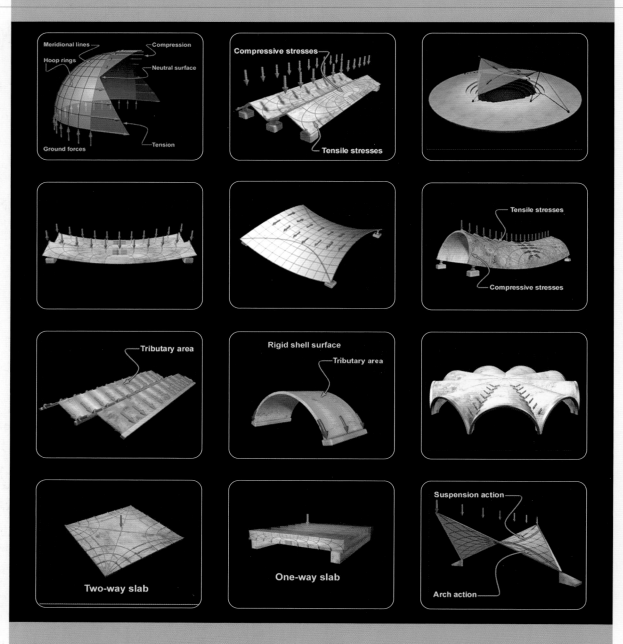

A Digital Pedagogy for Learning Structures

The Center of Visual Architecture at the University at Buffalo has undertaken an innovative new approach to teaching structures. **Shahin Vassigh**, Associate Professor in Structures, describes how the new programme she is developing at the school is imparting a new understanding of structural engineering and design.

Opposite
Screen shots of animations showing structural behaviour
(stress distribution and load-path diagrams) in surface
spanning systems

Below
In using this module, the student can begin by examining the work of an architect,
settling on a single work (building). Clicking on any part of the building structure
reveals the Basic Concepts of its structural design and the Structural Systems
used in its construction.

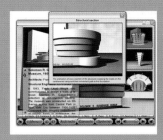

The practice of architecture is a delicate balance of art and science – a creative endeavour which also requires that the architect master a broad array of technical skills, including engineering. Educators teaching architecture therefore face a number of challenges in preparing their students for the demands of the profession. One of the most difficult problems shared by almost all architecture programmes is how to effectively teach architecture students the science of structural engineering and design. Although understanding structures is central to the education of the architect, the content and methods used to teach it are inappropriate for the vast majority of architecture students who need to know it.

Many instructors involved in teaching structures within architecture programmes would agree that the traditional methods for teaching structures to architecture students have many shortcomings. This is common, as significant parts of the curriculum and teaching methods are borrowed wholesale from engineering programmes. Most architecture students have limited mathematics skills yet are more often than not taught structures using a traditional engineering-based method which uses an abstract and diagrammatic approach to structural analysis, communicating even basic concepts with a high-level mathematics nomenclature. Teaching structures this way not only fails to provide students with an intuitive and conceptual grasp of the material but is also unrelated to the rest of the architecture curriculum.

The result is that many architecture students look at structures as a stale and incomprehensible subject matter that is merely a necessary requirement for graduation. Uninspired by an overly technical approach to structures, the majority of students consider the subject too difficult and irrelevant to the design and practice of architecture. By treating structures as the unwanted stepchild of the curriculum, the creative applications of structural design are left out of most design studios, and the students fail to see primary opportunities to reinforce structural concepts as design elements. Such neglect is carried into practice where architects produce designs that ignore structure out of fear of compromising the design or making it prohibitively costly in its execution.

Complex construction and advanced building design require a mastery of structures and construction technology. Inadequately prepared architecture graduates will compromise the quality of the built environment and will pose a clear risk to the professional practice of architecture. Modern building design and construction is highly interdisciplinary, requiring a mastery of applied structures in order to effectively manage the teams of technical personnel involved in the completion of the projects. Architecture students leave the academy poorly prepared to communicate and work with engineers. Professional architecture firms are then forced to invest in technical training to properly educate practising architects in the basics of structural design.

Faced with this recognised national deficiency in architecture education, many instructors are reconsidering how structures should be taught.

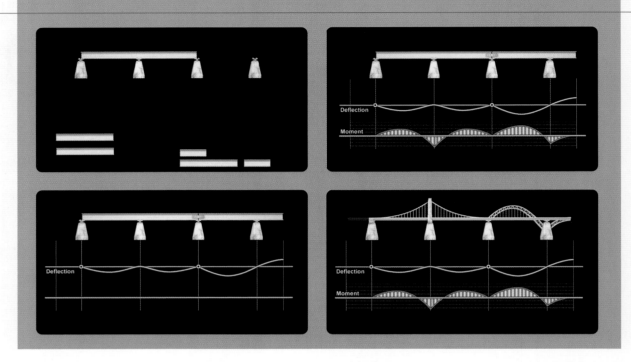

Although digital design tools have become a critical component of architecture education and practice in recent years, the potential for creating learning environments has been barely explored. Advances in computing technology have made it possible to develop innovative teaching methods that better meet the disposition and needs of architecture students.

Digital modelling combined with other advanced computer-graphics applications can be powerful tools in creating effective learning environments. Customised teaching environments can be created that demonstrate complex concepts with detailed and realistic visuals and graphics that are easy to understand. For example, in teaching structural analysis, virtual environments can be designed and manipulated to emphasise or de-emphasise certain structural or material properties. Material behaviour that is not visible at a large scale can be exaggerated to convey certain principles. Stress levels in a beam, deformation of a structural frame or the seismic behaviour of a certain building configuration can all become visually accessible. These environments can become interactive to maximise the user's engagement in the learning process. Structural components in a system can be removed or added to clarify the analysis, load travel path diagrams can be animated to demonstrate how the load is collected and distributed in a structural system and numerical analysis can be linked directly to the building context with realistic graphics and digital models.

Under a project supported by the US Department of Education, the Fund for the Improvement of Postsecondary Education (FIPSE)[1] faculty at the University at Buffalo is in the final stages of developing a project that utilises such a learning environment. The 'Interactive Structures Book' is a software package and a teaching tool that uses a wide range of digital and graphic technologies, including detailed and realistic 3-D computer-generated models, animations and audio narration,

to teach basic structural principles. The visual approach used in the development of this tool aims at promoting an intuitive understanding supported through the visualisation of structural behaviour. The software attempts to engage the students in studying architectural form in relation to structural behaviour and create awareness in the selection of form in light of structural function.

Although the work and methods for developing the software are new, they build on the work of significant authors and educators such as Mario Salvadori,[2] Heino Engel,[3] Daniel Schodek,[4] Ronald Shaeffer[5] and Waclaw Zalewski and Edward Allen.[6]

The full version of the software divides the study of structures into three modules: Basic Concepts, exploring general structural concepts, definitions and working principles; Structural Systems, a searchable database of structural subsystems (trusses, cables, arches, beams and columns, etc), construction details and models of structural behaviour; and Architects, a searchable and interactive database of significant works of prominent architects, presented using computer-generated models, photographs, films and interactive files.

The primary learning element of the software is that each area is not a separate study module but a point from which to initiate different aspects of structural performance and analysis. For example, a user can examine the work of an architect by interacting with a selected structure. Clicking on any part of the building structure reveals the Basic Concepts of its structural design and the Structural Systems utilised in its construction. Through the use of linked menus and

Left
Load-path distribution for the roof of the Renault Distribution Center
Norman Foster and Associates, Swindon, England, 1982
Key frames from the animation show the load-distribution path in the roof system. The animation
helps students understand the hierarchy of structural elements in receiving and distributing loads.

Right
Load-path distribution for the roof of the Palace of Labor
Nervi and Bartoli, Turin, Italy, 1960
Key frames from the animation show how the steel-supported
roof slab collects loads and moves them to the central column.

hypertext, all concept areas are linked and accessible from within each other. A complete building provides a visual access that grounds the investigation. Successive layers of information (mathematical formulas, analytical results, graphic representations of behaviour, etc) can be accessed and used to overlay the buildings. Rather than abstract representations, 3-D graphics are used and most are animated to simulate behaviour under stress. Using specific methods, the following sections discuss how the software can be used to assist students learning structures in the context of architectural design relevant to their daily educational experience.

The project has been tested and evaluated at the University at Buffalo and the University of Oregon. While almost all students have shown improvement when compared to classes taught using traditional methods, there has been a significantly greater improvement in grades among the female students (of about 6.3 per cent) with a somewhat smaller improvement among the male students. Student feedback on various surveys has ranged from 'neat graphics', 'keeps me from falling sleep' to 'a helpful tool to learn structures'.

Structural Origins of Form
Typically, studying the variation of forces and moments in a structural member is a critical component of teaching structures. In most structures courses, this is achieved through numerical exercises that involve longhand calculations of the internal forces and moments, followed by plotting shear and moment diagrams. The final stage of this exercise is the design of the structural member. In structural engineering terms, this means selecting the most economical member that performs the structural function safely.

Although this is a very important exercise in analysing structural behaviour, it fails to go beyond a quantitative exercise.

This exercise could be significantly improved if the relationship of the architectural form, moment diagram and deflection mechanism of a structure or structural member were explored simultaneously. In the Interactive Structures Book, this is accomplished by interactive examples. In one exercise, students are given a set of components that can be assembled into a bridge. Once completed, the software generates moment and deflection diagrams and a structural form in direct response to the applied stresses.

The key learning element of the interactive examples is that users can achieve different results with consecutive tries and learn by comparing these results. With the help of similar exercises it is likely to change the students' conceptions of drawing moment diagrams from a useless, laborious effort to a potential form of expression in the process of architectural design.

Visualising Load Travel Paths
Many structural engineering computer programs designed for performing analytical calculations have some visualisation capability for showing structural response under the load application. Although architecture students could potentially benefit from the use of these programs, their use requires an extensive knowledge of structural concepts, careful engineering modelling skills and proper assumptions and procedures for load application to the models. Although they have become more intelligible, the programs are exclusively tailored for the use of engineers and notably difficult for architecture students to use. Even when architecture students learn to use the programs, they can only engage them at an elementary level and

Below
Details in context, Channel Tunnel Railway Terminal
Nicholas Grimshaw & Partners, Waterloo, London, 1993
Screen shots of animations showing how students can investigate
the details of the structure in the overall context of the building.

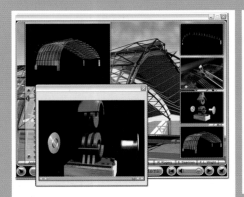
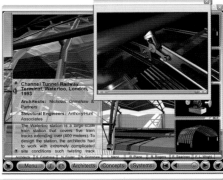
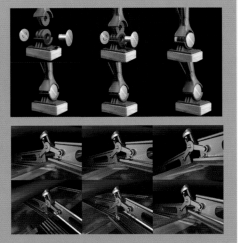

cannot relate them to complex architectural structures.

Considering the importance of visualisation to the understanding of structural behaviour, the Interactive Structures Book utilises digital building models to show the load-collection mechanism and load-distribution path across the entire structural system. Animated load-path diagrams of the entire structure can help students comprehend the hierarchy of structural elements in receiving and distributing loads far more effectively than is possible with static diagrams.

Context As a Learning Environment

A significant portion of architectural education is based on studying precedents and examining the work of various architects and landmark buildings. Although many faculties that teach structures use the analysis of existing buildings as a venue for discussion, the effectiveness of their effort is limited by the constraints of the traditional delivery system of information. Most often, case studies cannot go beyond a standard analysis, which includes a few static images or graphical representations of the building (or building components) followed by diagrams and mathematical annotations. To enhance the effectiveness of this approach, the Interactive Structures Book uses digital tools to transform case studies into interactive learning environments. The possibility of moving through the building and exposing structural elements deliberately selected by the user engages the entire building as a context, rather than merely a particular aspect of the building. In addition, the digital models permit focusing on details as well as the entire structure simultaneously, therefore clearly connecting the detail to the whole and vice versa.

Closing Remarks

Improving the teaching of structures in architecture programmes is essential for the practice of architecture. The various subdisciplines of the profession have become increasingly fragmented over recent decades as buildings and their component systems have grown more complex. In order

for architects to be able to co-ordinate the design of a complex building they must have a sound understanding of its component systems. Since the structure of a building is so intimately linked to its form, an architect with a limited understanding of structure will be severely compromised in his or her ability to work in the field.

The central underlying principle for the development of the described project is to provide a learning environment designed to accommodate the thinking, strengths and interests of architecture students. The Interactive Structures Book uses state-of-the-art digital graphics and animations to provide a visual and direct means of communicating concepts, grounding them in a real-world context. The initial evaluation of the student performance has indicated that this means of communication is extremely effective. As the potential of digital learning environments is steadily increasing with advancing technology, projects such as this can be further enhanced and become more powerful. △

Notes
1 The project is composed of three components: the 'Interactive Structures Book'; an instructional support centre website (the 'Structures Learning Center' at www.learningstructures.org); and student performance evaluation tools. The project is currently under testing and evaluation at the University at Buffalo, the State University of New York and the University of Oregon.
2 Mario Salvadori, *Structures in Architecture: The Building of Buildings*, Prentice Hall (New Jersey), 1986.
3 Heino Engel, *Structures Systems*, Deutsche Verlags-Anstalt GmbH (Stuttagart), 1967.
4 Daniel Schodek, *Structures*, fourth edition, Prentice Hall (Ohio), 2001.
5 Ronald Shaeffer, *Elementary Structures for Architects and Builders*, third edition, Prentice Hall (Ohio), 1988.
6 Waclaw Zalewski and Edward Allen, *Shaping Structures*, John Wiley and Sons (New York), 1998.

Shahin Vassigh is an associate professor of structures and the co-director of the Center for Virtual Architecture at the University at Buffalo, the State University of New York. She has a wide range of experience in structural engineering as well as teaching structures. Her research focuses on structural and architectural design, and on the application of digital media to structural pedagogy and instructional materials. For further information on learning structures see www.learningstructures.org or contact Vassigh by email at vassigh@ap.buffalo.edu.

Below
Hybrid Border Postcard, photo-collage of US/Mexico border zone, Ana Alemán, et al, LA/LA Studio, 2000.

estudio
teddy cruz

Denise Bratton relates how Teddy Cruz is realising his vision of the US/Mexican border zone as a testing ground for radical urban strategies. Through a series of collaborations with nonprofit community service agencies and enlightened clients that have emerged as powerful developers in their own communities, Cruz advocates urban complexity, hybridity and simultaneity in opposition to the sterile sub-urbanity that threatens to extinguish these conditions everywhere.

117+

Below
The US/Mexico border wall at Tijuana is emblematic of discriminating policies of segregation and control, but it is also the site of daily transgression. As capital, material resources and labour flow legally and illegally over the wall in countless round-trip exchanges, an urban landscape of contradiction emerges on both sides of the border, where conditions of sameness and difference collide and overlap.

A series of deliriously Hybrid Border Postcards published in the summer 1999 issue of *Architectural Design* on 'Architecture of the Borderlands'[1] strikingly prefigured recent projects by estudio teddy cruz for housing and community centres in densely occupied neighbourhoods of San Diego, California. In an essay on the Tijuana Workshop he directed at SCI-Arc in Los Angeles, Cruz described these dizzying images of the border zone, where San Diego meets Tijuana, as 'tools to reveal that which is hidden' in the urban fabric, 'fictional landscapes, fields of observation and infrastructure, photographically stitched out of the vacant spaces'. Mirroring the urbanistic potential of vacant places, the Border Postcards represent a hypothetical dynamic space 'ready to be occupied and activated by other narratives and events'.

Cruz's utopian agenda was clear: this was a manifesto on densification, proposing that fragments, voids and leftover urban spaces created by zoning and transport infrastructure could be transformed to support hybrid and layered programmes for flexible, affordable residential units, retail, commercial and green spaces. The goal was to achieve maximum effect with minimal gestures, to take existing patterns of use as a point of departure and to develop urban solutions with enough persuasive force to change obsolete planning policy and zoning regulations.

Not surprisingly, projects by estudio teddy cruz began to pivot on the axis of problems explored in the Tijuana Workshop as well as Latin America/Los Angeles (LA/LA), an international studio Cruz directed at SCI-Arc from 1994 to 2000. Using the border zone as a laboratory, intently observing thriving conditions in existing neighbourhoods and training a focus on underutilised elements of the urban infrastructure, Cruz has developed design solutions rooted in the specificity of individual communities and places. The objective is to distil the essence of patterns of use and to let these become the basis for incremental design solutions that have a catalytic effect on the urban fabric. Such a tactical approach generates prototypical solutions and perhaps paradigms for densification in cities elsewhere.

The generative paradox that engages Cruz and his team is the border itself – a shape-shifting imaginary line now engraved in the land with a 10-foot-high steel wall, a zone of frenzied interaction and exchange, an invitation to transgression, a threshold, an opening to new possibilities – but also an obstacle, a shield constructed to prevent their realisation, an opaque glass through which each side sees the other darkly. This boundary between two starkly different cultures and economies is blurred by the vast congested territory beginning at zero setback on the Mexican side and spilling into a no-man's-land northward on the US side. It is a place where the desire for porosity fuels humongous infrastructure systems while security is continually tightened to close the gaps.

Intensified global trade and population explosions on both sides of the border ensure that Tijuana and San Diego will undergo massive transformation in the 21st century as a result of global forces that converge in Southern California. Instead of repressing the tensions generated by this clash of contradictory forces, Cruz has drawn them to the surface, riveting international attention (positive as well as negative) on the question of how cities in the border zone will respond to the need to densify when the horizon of suburban sprawl is finally foreclosed, and the pristine and picturesque urbanism cultivated in affluent neighbourhoods proves incapable of meeting the needs of growing numbers of residents.

As if in parallel yet separate worlds, San Diego neighbourhoods such as San Ysidro and City Heights, where population densities are high, incomes are low and around 40 per cent of residents do not own cars (places seemingly forgotten by the greater municipality), coexist with gated communities of lesser density, higher income levels and greater demand for privacy, security and parking. And not to forget that 25 minutes from downtown San Diego lies the Mexican border town of Tijuana, notoriously wrongly perceived as decadent and lawless, impoverished and urbanistically backward. What Cruz calls a 'puritan' urbanism (driven by a desire for homogenised architectural styles and exclusionary planning practices) has resulted in zoning for San Diego that

dio teddy cruz estudio teddy cruz estudio teddy cruz estudio teddy cruz estudio teddy cruz estudio teddy cruz estudio teddy cruz estudio teddy cruz estudio teddy
teddy cruz estudio teddy cruz estudio teddy cruz estudio teddy cruz estudio teddy cruz estudio teddy cruz estudio teddy cruz estudio teddy cruz estudio teddy cruz estudio teddy
teddy cruz estudio teddy cruz estudio teddy cruz estudio teddy cruz estudio teddy cruz estudio teddy cruz estudio teddy cruz estudio teddy cruz estudio teddy cruz estudio
teddy cruz estudio teddy cruz estudio teddy cruz estudio teddy cruz estudio teddy cruz estudio teddy cruz estudio teddy cruz estudio teddy cruz estudio teddy

Living Rooms at the Border for Casa Familiar, San Ysidro, San Diego

Left
Sketches of layers 1, 2 and 3 showing three main phases of development across time.

Right
Model showing the juxtaposition of programmatic layers that create the overall composition, with arcades becoming infrastructure for the insertion of affordable housing.

Bottom
Perspective sketch showing remodelled 1927 church with Casa Familiar offices in the attic floor, affordable housing above market arcades and a community garden corridor in between.

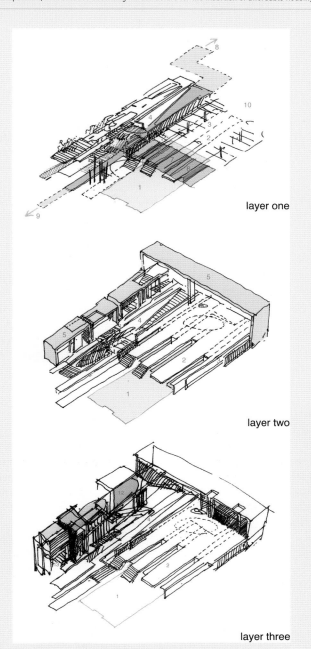

layer one

layer two

layer three

Living Rooms at the Border for Casa Familiar, San Ysidro, San Diego (begun 2000); PA Award 2001

The project focuses on strengthening a network of underused alleys and narrow streets, increasing pedestrian circulation and linking residential units with a park and a major tram station serving the border. A historic 1927 church is currently surrounded by parking on the existing site. Supported by public housing funds and private grants, Living Rooms at the Border will transform the parcel in increments, unfolding in time as community programmes are funded and further parcels become available. The programme has been conceived in three principal phases or 'layers'. The first (2001) encompasses the transformation of the church into a community centre (with new offices for Casa Familiar on the attic floor) and the creation of a community garden corridor. Extending these gestures that inscribe into the site new infrastructure and circulation corridors, the second phase (2003) will add poured-in-place concrete arcades to support flexible 'urban rooms' or pavilions for community activities. Opening on to the public garden, the arcades also generate space for a provisional market. In the third phase (2009), the concrete frame of the arbour will be built out with 12 flexible, affordable, wood-frame housing units.

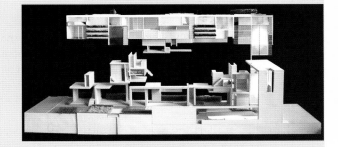

estudio teddy cruz estudio teddy cruz

opposes the forces and influences arising out of this continually changing and expanding 'border condition'; he advocates instead an urbanism of juxtaposition which embraces the carnivalesque and chaotic aspects of Tijuana and attends to the fine nuances of intensely layered programmes.

For almost a decade, in his teaching and practice Cruz has trained a hard focus on precisely this issue. He conceives the city as a collection of inert fragments waiting to be activated through synergistic development, their potential residing in a certain contingency rather than cure-all master planning. What galvanises Cruz's practice is the conviction that lessons can be learnt from the 'great bi-national metropolis' stretching from San Diego to Tijuana, where radically different economic and cultural spheres clash and overlap as they embrace recurring waves of immigrants from around the world. He sees in this condition the promise of an urbanism that admits the full spectrum of social and spatial possibility.

The collaborative team of estudio teddy cruz, more policy- than design-oriented, dedicates itself to the challenges of the present, to projects conceived – both practically and philosophically – as multiphase operations that address their particular requirements and purposes but which, like the Trojan Horse, when they are 'unpacked' in the city tend to alter the course of future development. The studio has sought out projects for affordable mixed-use housing developments in communities where extended multi-family households predominate, studying ad-hoc urban solutions in neighbourhoods where residents and small-business owners have appropriated patterns of use and habitations typical throughout Latin America and the Caribbean region. Take the *callejón*, or alley, for example. This humble and ubiquitous element of the urban fabric morphs into a generator of flexible spaces in the hands of estudio teddy cruz, whose novel solutions reinforce the use of pedestrian accessways typically stigmatised by urban planners, and thus reinforce their inherent capacity to support overlapping programmes and landscaped spaces.

Cruz's modest approach is betrayed by the farsightedness of his agenda, which has led him to collaborate with influential nonprofit community service agencies embedded in the neighbourhoods of San Diego. Following the lead of architect-developers such as Ted Smith (Smith and Others), whose affordable housing ventures have brought San Diego considerable notoriety, these nonprofits have emerged as a self-organising force, becoming developers in their own communities and dealing implicitly with an insurgent urbanism that pushes the envelope of existing zoning. Cruz has teamed up with two of the most prominent, Casa Familiar and La Maestra. Founded in 1972 to provide basic services to Spanish-speaking immigrants in greater San Diego, Casa Familiar now serves all racial and ethnic groups. From a single bungalow that functioned as a multipurpose drop-in centre, the organisation broadened its reach to provide educational programmes, housing services and economic development,

its larger mission being the economic revitalisation of the historic core of San Ysidro.

estudio teddy cruz has designed two award-winning multiphase projects for Casa Familiar. With Living Rooms at the Border (begun 2000), client and architect conspired to put San Ysidro back on San Diego's radar screen. The project focuses on open-ended housing and live-work solutions for typical residents. Sited on a parcel zoned for no more than three housing units, it is now slated for subdivision into a proposed 12 highly flexible affordable housing units plus offices for Casa Familiar, with public gardens, a market and other provisional uses. Neither the subdivision (a two-bedroom unit, for example, can be divided into two small studios sharing a kitchen) nor the mixed-use is allowed under existing zoning, but the project is moving forward on the strength of its pioneering combination of desirable and sustainable mixed-uses.

Senior Gardens – Housing with Childcare is another project inspired by Casa Familiar's distinctive cultural values and attitudes towards domestic and public space. Focusing on bringing two generations together, the central elements of the programme are affordable housing for seniors and grandchildren (a form of cohabitation common in this area of the city) and daycare facilities for children with working parents. The programme has been distilled into a system of layers in which private and public spaces are interwoven with the topography of the site. Cruz's design is considered to be prototypical, another provocative instrument through which Casa Familiar hopes to redefine setback, land-use and density requirements.

Likewise, La Maestra, a nonprofit family clinic founded in 1991 to provide primary healthcare for low-income residents of City Heights, one of San Diego's most diverse neighbourhoods, started small but has grown with burgeoning immigrant populations in need of such services. Cruz's project for the La Maestra Family Clinic was launched in 2001, its design inspired by existing site conditions: alleys informally used as a network of pedestrian paths, and narrow streets connecting pedestrian alleys with Imperial Avenue. The project stimulates commercial and social activity perpendicular to a major transport corridor and heightens the complexity and interest of activity within the site itself.

As their engagement with particular neighbourhoods has deepened, Casa Familiar and La Maestra have expanded their goals to include building housing tailored to the social and cultural make-up of the communities they serve. Their collaboration with estudio teddy cruz has produced architecture mindful of the need for a certain quality of life, pride in one's home and the public space and parks of the

Senior Gardens – Housing with Childcare for Casa Familiar, San Ysidro, San Diego

Top and middle left
Sketch and pattern diagrams showing the project as programmatic 'stripes' in the context of the existing built fabric of loose, detached single-family dwellings, with alternating sloping roof planes visually integrated into the multiple programmatic conditions on the ground.

Middle right
Aerial view of model showing the alternating rhythm of slender building blocks and linear gardens.

Bottom
View showing the relation between the living unit and the private garden.

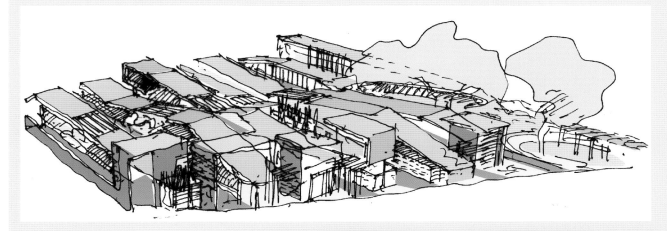

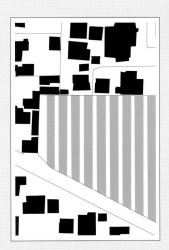

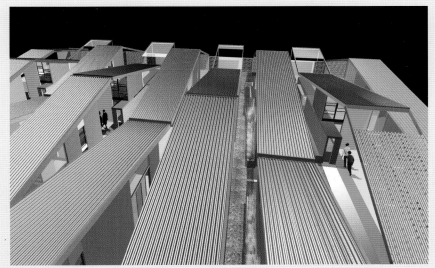

Senior Gardens – Housing with Childcare for Casa Familiar, San Ysidro, San Diego (begun 2002); AIA Merit Award 2003

Comprising 14 affordable housing units of 600 to 1,000 square feet, and six studios of about 400 square feet, the programme is particularly sensitive to the special social and emotional needs of elderly members of this community. Private access to each unit, both from a main entrance in a private garden that opens on to a communal garden promenade, and from the alley, has been provided. Senior housing is also closely linked to the childcare facility, with access via the communal promenade that also connects this project to Casa Familiar's other housing developments in San Ysidro. The repetition of standardised elements such as service walls containing kitchens, bathrooms and storage space is interrupted by a variety of roof-line configurations and gardens to strengthen the spatial flow among housing units, and each kitchen has the flexibility to open on to the promenade, creating an ad-hoc communal social space as desired. Studio loft apartments perched above and behind some of the units have separate entrances so that they can be independently occupied by extended family and friends or rented out.

estudio teddy cruz estudio

La Maestra Family Clinic, City Heights, San Diego

Top left
Flow diagram showing the system of interwoven circulation paths that blur distinctions between public and private space.

Top right
Ramp gardens

Bottom
Market.

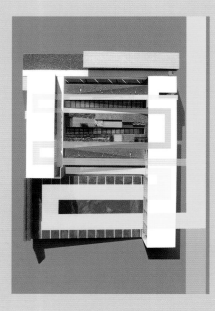

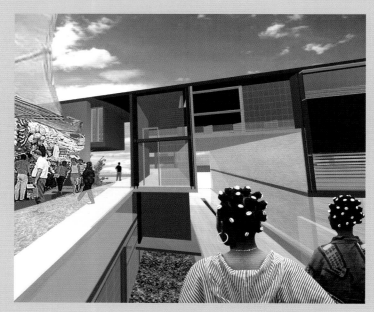

La Maestra Family Clinic, City Heights/San Diego (begun 2001)

The clinic will be located along Fairmount Avenue, flanked by El Cajon Boulevard and University Avenue – two of San Diego's most vital urban corridors. Proposed elements include a new outpatient clinic and administrative offices, a parking structure and community rooms. The various elements are designed to take advantage of the structure's multiple levels and roof space in order to satisfy parking requirements and induce pedestrian circulation. The roof is conceived as a network of landscaped terraces and garden ramps that connect levels devoted to the clinic and other La Maestra community services, retail shops, offices and parking. These garden ramps double as the site for community activities, with light pavilions to shelter outdoor markets, musical events and neighbourhood festivals. Conceived in generatve phases that anticipate La Maestra's future development of the rest of the block, the project proposes an alternating system of linear gardens, passageways and buildings. In the first phase, four parcels surrounded by existing alleys are being developed along the boulevard.

neighbourhood, and economic viability for small retail and business enterprises. Clearly, sustained engagement with specific communities has privileged Casa Familiar and La Maestra with insight that municipal planners and commercial developers do not necessarily possess; thus, planning in their hands is driven by cultural and site specificity rather than the proverbial bottom line.

The logical next step is to turn this accumulated knowledge into policy by proving 'on the ground' that nonprofit developers with definite social agendas are capable of 'growing' communities that possess a strong civic sense. Urban interventions are envisioned as part of long-term commitment to neighbourhoods: small projects that acknowledge the histories and identities of culturally specific communities; collaborations involving architects, nonprofit developers, city planners and other agencies; transformations of modest idiosyncratic parcels to create space in which small economies can flourish; and phased redevelopment efforts that allow communities to adapt, personalise and transform spaces to fit their needs and means.

Cruz has entered into equally fruitful collaborations with private developers, as in the project for Housing Corridors on Imperial Avenue in Logan Heights (begun 2002). Here, again, the point of departure was the existing dense, older urban fabric consisting of alleys informally used as pedestrian corridors and narrow

Housing Corridors on Imperial Avenue, Logan Heights, San Diego
Top left
View of landscaped corridor giving access to living units while acting as
passageway from alley to boulevard

Top right
Aerial view of living unit bays, creating an alternating rhythm of property-wall planes and interstitial gardens.

Bottom
Front elevation of living units showing a vertical rhythm of occluded and porous conditions.

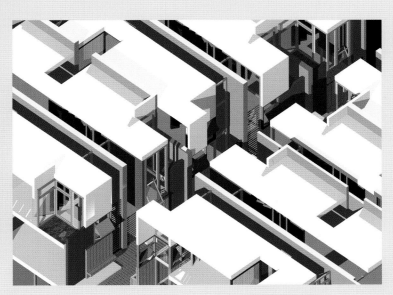

**Housing Corridors on Imperial Avenue, Logan Heights, San Diego
(begun 2002); AIA Honor Award, 2002**
This project involves the hybrid development of six parcels, combining 58
affordable housing units with 9,000 square feet of small-retail space. Five of
the parcels will be built in the first phase, and the sixth incorporated later on.
One of the challenges was to project a pattern of density that could anticipate
the sixth plot's inclusion but read as a 'whole' in the meantime. The pattern
resulted from close observation of the character of the existing fabric: small
streets have been reinvented as landscaped passages that allow the
interlocking of residential and small retail and reinforce pedestrian movement.
Housing and retail spaces envelop parking garages, rendering them invisible
from the street but accessible from the alleys. Passages above the parking
become elevated garden streets giving private access to individual units,
while those at ground level give access to commercial and live-work galleries.
Units are designed as flexible frames that can accommodate a range of
configurations including studio, one-, two- and three-bedroom apartments,
live-work lofts or retail shops, and are layered in double-height vertical bays
delineated by balconies and patios leading to private roof gardens.

streets supporting small retail and commercial
establishments with housing above – all bounded
by one of the most vital urban corridors in the city:
Imperial Avenue. The design, derived from the pattern
of the street network, proposes an extension of
existing mixed-use, which is technically nonconforming
according to existing zoning but dynamically effective
in the community.

The logic of the architectural solutions that Cruz
is devising is already being recognised by the
municipality of San Diego. As Cruz noted in a recent
article in *C3 Views*, the journal of the organisation
Citizens Coordinate for Century 3: 'Currently, city
planning projects like "City of Villages" are trying
to revise and critique existing zoning conditions …
realizing the need for more flexible zoning policies
that can promote the appropriate mixed uses and
quality densification within certain communities.
It is in communities like San Ysidro where the
vitality of existing patterns of use begin to generate
a particular kind of urbanism from within.'[2] ⚙

Notes
1 Teddy Cruz, 'Tijuana Workshop – Border Chronicles of a Vertical Studio at SCI-Arc',
in Teddy Cruz and Anne Boddington (eds), 'Architecture of the Borderlands',
Architectural Design 69, July/August 1999, pp 42–7.
2 Teddy Cruz, 'Surgical Urbanism in San Ysidro', *C3 Views*, July–August 2002, p 6.

Denise Bratton is an art and architectural historian, editor and publishing
consultant, and a member of the editorial board of *Architectural Design*.

Below
estudio teddy cruz: Teddy Cruz (left), Giacomo Castagnola, Adriana Cuéllar,
Mariana Leguía, Alan Rosenblum, Jota (José Jaime) Samper and Jess Field.

Résumé

estudio teddy cruz

1979–82	BA, Rafael Landivar University, Guatemala City
1984–9	Project Designer, Pacific Associates Planners & Architects, San Diego
1985	Master plan of Civic Center and City Hall, Escondido, California
	Home Sweet Home Residence, San Diego
1986	PA Award for Home Sweet Home Residence
1986–7	California State University International Program, Florence
1987	BArch, California State Polytechnic University, San Luis Obispo
	MDesS, Harvard University Graduate School of Design
1988	Master plan of Civic Center, Moreno Valley, California
1989–93	Project designer, Rob Wellington Quigley, FAIA, San Diego
1989	Sherman Heights Community Center, San Diego
	Capistrano Beach Residence
	AIA, San Diego Chapter, Merit Award for Capistrano Beach Residence
1990	Fallbrook Residence, San Diego
1991	Extraordinary Desserts Café, San Diego
	Rome Prize, American Academy in Rome
	Solana Beach Amtrak Station
	Municipal Gymnasium, Balboa Park, San Diego
1991–5	Adjunct professor, New School of Architecture, San Diego
1992	St Davis Episcopal Church, San Diego
1993	Founder, estudio teddy cruz
	Las Gradas Residence, Tijuana, Mexico
1993–2000	Design faculty, SCI-Arc, Los Angeles
1994–2000	Founder, Latin America/Los Angeles (LA/LA)Studio, SCI-Arc, Los Angeles
1994	AIA, San Diego Chapter, Honor Award for Las Gradas Residence
1995	Visiting Fellow, California State Polytechnic University, San Luis Obispo
1996	San Diego Public Library
1998	Assistant professor, Woodbury University, San Diego Campus
	Chair, Mundaneum – International Conference on Architecture, Costa Rica
1999	Chair, Reinventing Tijuana Conference, IMPlan, Tijuana, Mexico
	Guest editor, with Anne Boddington, 'Architecture of the Borderlands', *AD* Six Row Houses, Tijuana, Mexico
2000	Chair, 5th International Conference of Architectural Educators, ITESM, Mexico City
	Adviser, 2nd Mies van der Rohe Award for Latin American Architecture
	Rubalcaba-Klink Residence, San Diego
	Living Rooms at the Border for Casa Familiar, San Ysidro, San Diego
2001	PA Award for Living Rooms at the Border, San Ysidro, San Diego
	Co-chair, Hot Topics Committee, Council of Design Professionals, City of San Diego
	La Maestra Family Clinic, City Heights, San Diego
	Centro Cultural de la Raza, San Diego
	AIA, San Diego Chapter, Merit Award for Rubalcaba-Klink Residence
	Architectural League of New York, Young Architects Forum Award
2002	Member, Public Art Master Plan Steering Committee, City of San Diego
	Senior Gardens – Housing with Childcare for Casa Familiar, San Ysidro, San Diego
	Housing Corridors on Imperial Avenue, Logan Heights, San Diego
	AIA Honor Award for Housing Corridors on Imperial Avenue, Logan Heights, San Diego
2003	Garden Terraces on Mildred Avenue, Linda Vista, San Diego
	AIA Merit Award for Garden Terraces on Mildred Avenue, Linda Vista, San Diego
	AIA Merit Award for Senior Gardens – Housing with Childcare, San Ysidro, San Diego
	P4 – Sewer Pump Station #4, Inter-Agency Public Art Collaboration, City of San Diego

◭ Book Club
Architectural Design

Get inspired – with these fantastic offers on a range of Wiley-Academy's innovative design titles

Confessions: Principles Architecture Process Life
Jan Kaplicky
Confessions offers an insight into the mind of Future Systems architect Jan Kaplicky – his ideas, opinions and sources of inspiration. With an equal balance of images and textual observations, it is both visually and mentally engaging, and is an incredibly personal and honest account.

0-471-49541-7; 204pp; August 2002; Paperback; £24.95 £14.97

The Four States of Architecture
Hanrahan + Meyers Architects
The first book to chart the talent of exceptional New York firm, Hanrahan + Meyers, with support, via written contributions, from key figures such as Robert Stern and Bernard Tschumi

0-471-49652-9; 128pp; April 2002; Paperback; £24.95 £14.97

Sustaining Architecture in the Anti-Machine Age
Ian Abley
This book brings together contributions from a range of architects, journalists, academics and consultants, approaching sustainability from a wide variety of viewpoints. Each chapter includes a robust, lively text, illustrated with carefully chosen exemplar projects.

0-471-48660-4; 240pp January 2002; Paperback; £19.99 £11.99

First House
Christian Bjone
Covers the first works of a group of key architects who were teaching and/or studying at Harvard between the late 1930s and the early 1950s. Includes first houses by Gropius and Breuer, Ulrich Franzen, Philip Johnson, Paul Rudolph and IM Pei
"...beautifully produced clever and thoughtful..."
—**The Twentieth-Century Society Newsletter**

0-470-84538-4; 224pp; April 2002; Hardback; £39.95 £23.97

Archi-toons: Funniness, Comedy and Delight
Richard T Bynum
Explore the lighter side of architecture with this volume of humorous cartoons from the internationally renowned architect and popular cartoonist and illustrator Rick Bynum. These cartoons take a quirky, witty, insightful and sometimes irreverent look at the world of design, architecture and construction.

0-470-85406-5; 128pp; April 2003; Paperback; £9.99 £6.00

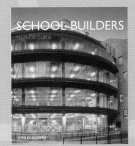

School Builders
Eleanor Curtis
School Builders provides a fascinating overview of the latest developments in school design from around the world. Packed with construction methods, case studies, outstanding imagery and technical plans, it offers an indispensable guide for planning and designing school buildings, from primary through to high schools.

0-471-62377-6; 224pp; January 2003; Hardback; £50.00 £30.00

Encyclopaedia of Architectural Technology
Jacqueline Glass
A comprehensive guide to architectural technology, that encompasses every aspect of modern construction. Including several hundred entries in alphabetical order with diagrams and illustrations, this is an essential guide for the architect and student alike
"More than a mere dictionary of architectural terms...a useful reference tome with a detailed explanation of many key terms."
—**Architects Journal**

0-471-88559-2; 360pp; February 2002; Hardback; £60.00 £36.00

Save 40%
When you subscribe to Architectural Design you automatically become a member of the AD Book Club and become eligible for 40% discount on specially selected titles in each issue. These titles will range from the latest in architectural theory to strikingly illustrated guides to the funkiest interior design.

To launch this initiative, for one issue only, we are offering this incentive to all our readers, irrespective of whether they are subscribers, whilst in future the discount will be available exclusively to AD subscribers.

For further information call our Customer Services Department on +44 (0)1243 843294 or visit www.wileyeurope.com. Quote reference CVU when you order the above titles to claim your 40% discount. Offer ends 30th April 2004.

Light

Leon van Schaik
describes Stephen
Bram's Light
installation for
Liberty Tower
in Melbourne
which creates an
axis for debate
between artist
and space-makers.

Opposite
Stephen Bram's neon installation links the street-facing area of the foyer to the
rear lift-lobby area. The mirrored walls of the foyer reflect the street scene outside.

I last opened an exhibition of Stephen Bram's work at the Anna Schwartz gallery on 4 June 1996 – seven years ago. At the time I challenged the notion that the work was architectural although I noted a resonance between Bram's early spatial projects and the architecture of ARM's Royal Melbourne Institute of Technology (RMIT) Storey Hall (those non-periodic tiles). I suggested that the use of these tiles might descend from his earlier explorations. This notion discomforted him. Bram has been thinking and feeling his way through the relationship between his art and architecture very carefully in the intervening seven years. And it is a journey that gives pause.

I can now see that ARM's Storey Hall Gallery at RMIT represents for Bram the difficulties that arise when an architect makes an expressive space that impinges on the way artists and their work can play themselves out. As Bram's installation in Munich – Oberföhringer Strasse 156[1] – proves by itself manipulating gallery space, the architectural manipulations of gallery spaces remove from some artists the possibility of working in the modulations of spatiality. Bram's difficulties in working in the increasingly dramatically encoded spaces of galleries that express the architect's ordering systems (from Gehry to Hadid) have convinced him that a gallery is a space that has to have a certain neutrality.

Bram has sourced a 1986 text by Remy Zaugg that sets out a technical specification for gallery spaces now. It is titled 'The Art Museum I dream of, or The Place of the work and the People'. This is a plea for a place that speaks of artists and their art; it stands in opposition to places that speak of the work of architects and *their* work. It also argues its way to a new form of planning – the closing diagrams are of large rectangles filled with loosely related rooms – that has liberated galleries from the enfilade and service corridor model. But more of this later.

What, then, does the Light installation at Liberty Tower tell me? Here, Bram the artist works with a space with a supportively low architectural resistance. Ellenberg Fraser's foyer design is not playful. It is resolutely orthogonal. The walls are at right angles to the floor. The ceiling is at right angles to the walls. The walls are planes of a single material: slightly smoked mirror. The ceiling is a plane of a single material: white plaster. The floor is a plane of smoked charcoal granite. The plan is two rectangles approaching golden mean in proportion, slid apart to overlap only at the corners of their long walls, where they interlink – almost all in alignment with Zaugg's principles for a gallery room. But the chief architectural purpose of the foyer is to resolve a set of specific programmatic requirements: how to get from the front door to the lifts and on to the mailroom at the rear.

In this space, Bram hangs the three-dimensional Light, a neon frame based on the three-dimensional relationship between three points in space, which the camera moved towards and away from in his film *Kuala Lumpur 1998*. In some circumstances the interrelationship between such an inserted object and architecture creates decorative art, and the result is one voice. At Liberty Tower, the insertion is so ephemeral that at times when there is a dialogue and unity,

Light dominates completely. This is possible because the architecture is so minimal in its rhetoric. Perhaps an expressive space that demands a dialogue converts any insertion into decorative art.

According to Bram: 'On reading Zaugg's text, I recognised the architectural impediments to exhibition he describes as exactly the same as those that I (and I believe other artists who share certain similar concerns) face in our work. It's not so much that I believe that the architecture of the exhibition space should allow the autonomy of the work, in fact it's the contrary – it should allow something other than autonomy for the work, it should allow it to connect with the space, to function. If I have one criticism of Zaugg's text it is that this third term in the situation of the experience of the artwork is not explicitly enough stated. The exhibition space is partner to the work in the experience of the perceiver – the work is always seen/understood in relation to its architectural context.'[2]

This is a hard call on architects. Daniel Buren spatialises signs in the environment, but the environment brims with signifiers. Bram seeks to spatialise signs in environments, and environments that are not in themselves already signs of something else are rare, probably an impossibility. Zumthor's Bregenz is a neutral 'art-box' that tries to counter the chaotic, but even here the concrete of the walls and the glass of the ceilings give rise to a demanding dialogue so pressing that the only works that have survived are floor works.

Light at Liberty Tower floats easily in the crux of this debate between artist and space-makers. Ironically, through its reflections it becomes a piece of decorative art indistinguishable from the room within which it sits, as it ricochets away into the distance on all sides, and into infinity in some, setting up shimmers and shifts. And yet in this shimmering it goes beyond decorating the space and asserts its independent origin, and its independent existence as an idea.

Bram's practice alerts us to the probability that dialogue, like hybridisation, depends on difference. Light reveals the benefits of diverse practices, those of these architects and this artist. Paradoxically, however, Bram's discovery of Zaugg's prescriptions proves, despite my opening remarks, that artists do have some leadership role in spatial design. Zaugg – as I have indicated above – suggests a way of organising gallery plans that is now winning competitions around the world. Even if only through morphic resonance, Zaugg's 1986 diagrams are lineal antecedents to the plan created by Kazuyo Sejima and Ruye Nishizawa for their Contemporary Art Museum, Kanazawa (1999). ⌂

Notes
1 Stephen Bram, 'Oberföhringer Strasse 156', Poetics in Architecture, *Architectural Design*, vol 72, no 2, March 2002, p 84.
2 Email from Stephen Bram to Leon Van Schaik, 23 June 2003.

Subscribe Now

As an influential and prestigious architectural publication, *Architectural Design* has an almost unrivalled reputation worldwide. Published bimonthly, it successfully combines the currency and topicality of a newsstand journal with the editorial rigour and design qualities of a book. Consistently at the forefront of cultural thought and design since the 1960s, it has time and again proved provocative and inspirational – inspiring theoretical, creative and technological advances. Prominent in the 1980s for the part it played in Postmodernism and then in Deconstruction, ⟁ has recently taken a pioneering role in the technological revolution of the 1990s. With groundbreaking titles dealing with cyberspace and hypersurface architecture, it has pursued the conceptual and critical implications of high-end computer software and virtual realities. ⟁

⟁ Architectural Design

SUBSCRIPTION RATES 2004
Institutional Rate: UK £175
Personal Rate: UK £99
Discount Student* Rate: UK £70
OUTSIDE UK
Institutional Rate: US $270
Personal Rate: US $155
Student* Rate: US $110

*Proof of studentship will be required when placing an order. Prices reflect rates for a 2002 subscription and are subject to change without notice.

TO SUBSCRIBE
Phone your credit card order:
+44 (0)1243 843 828

Fax your credit card order to:
+44 (0)1243 770 432

Email your credit card order to:
cs-journals@wiley.co.uk

Post your credit card or cheque order to:
John Wiley & Sons Ltd.
Journals Administration Department
1 Oldlands Way
Bognor Regis
West Sussex PO22 9SA
UK

Please include your postal delivery address with your order.

All ⟁ volumes are available individually. To place an order please write to:
John Wiley & Sons Ltd
Customer Services
1 Oldlands Way
Bognor Regis
West Sussex PO22 9SA

Please quote the ISBN number of the issue(s) you are ordering.

⟁ is available to purchase on both a subscription basis and as individual volumes

○ I wish to subscribe to ⟁ *Architectural Design* at the **Institutional rate of £175**.

○ I wish to subscribe to ⟁ *Architectural Design* at the **Personal rate of £99**.

○ I wish to subscribe to ⟁ *Architectural Design* at the **Student rate of £70**.

○ ⟁ *Architectural Design* is available to individuals on either a calendar year or rolling annual basis; Institutional subscriptions are only available on a calendar year basis. Tick this box if you would like your Personal or Student subscription on a rolling annual basis.

○ Payment enclosed by Cheque/Money order/Drafts.

Value/Currency £/US$ _____

○ Please charge £/US$ _____ to my credit card.
Account number:

Expiry date:

Card: Visa/Amex/Mastercard/Eurocard *(delete as applicable)*

Cardholder's signature _____

Cardholder's name _____

Address _____

_____

_____ Post/Zip Code _____

Recipient's name _____

Address _____

_____

_____ Post/Zip Code _____

I would like to buy the following issues at £22.50 each:

○ ⟁ 167 *Property Development*, David Sokol
○ ⟁ 166 *Club Culture*, Eleanor Curtis
○ ⟁ 165 *Urban Flashes Asia*, Nicholas Boyarsky + Peter Lang
○ ⟁ 164 *Home Front: New Developments in Housing*, Lucy Bullivant
○ ⟁ 163 *Art + Architecture*, Ivan Margolius
○ ⟁ 162 *Surface Consciousness*, Mark Taylor
○ ⟁ 161 *Off the Radar*, Brian Carter + Annette LeCuyer
○ ⟁ 160 *Food + Architecture*, Karen A Franck
○ ⟁ 159 *Versioning in Architecture*, SHoP
○ ⟁ 158 *Furniture + Architecture*, Edwin Heathcote
○ ⟁ 157 *Reflexive Architecture*, Neil Spiller
○ ⟁ 156 *Poetics in Architecture*, Leon van Schaik
○ ⟁ 155 *Contemporary Techniques in Architecture*, Ali Rahim
○ ⟁ 154 *Fame and Architecture*, J. Chance and T. Schmiedeknecht
○ ⟁ 153 *Looking Back in Envy*, Jan Kaplicky
○ ⟁ 152 *Green Architecture*, Brian Edwards
○ ⟁ 151 *New Babylonians*, Iain Borden + Sandy McCreery
○ ⟁ 150 *Architecture + Animation*, Bob Fear
○ ⟁ 149 *Young Blood*, Neil Spiller
○ ⟁ 148 *Fashion and Architecture*, Martin Pawley
○ ⟁ 147 *The Tragic in Architecture*, Richard Patterson
○ ⟁ 146 *The Transformable House*, Jonathan Bell and Sally Godwin
○ ⟁ 145 *Contemporary Processes in Architecture*, Ali Rahim
○ ⟁ 144 *Space Architecture*, Dr Rachel Armstrong
○ ⟁ 143 *Architecture and Film II*, Bob Fear
○ ⟁ 142 *Millennium Architecture*, Maggie Toy and Charles Jencks